DESEGREGATION
IN AMERICAN
SCHOOLS

DESEGREGATION IN AMERICAN SCHOOLS

Comparative Intervention
Strategies

BRIAN L. FIFE

New York
Westport, Connecticut
London

Library of Congress Cataloging-in-Publication Data

Fife, Brian L.
   Desegregation in American schools : comparative intervention
strategies / Brian L. Fife.
      p. cm.
   Includes bibliographical references and index.
   ISBN 0-275-94140-X
   1. School integration—United States—Case studies.
   2. Educational equalization—United States—Case studies.
   I. Title.
   LC214.32.F54   1992
   370.19′342—dc20   91-33163

British Library Cataloguing in Publication Data is available.

Library of Congress Catalog Card Number: 91-33163
ISBN: 0-275-94140-X

First published in 1992

Praeger Publishers, One Madison Avenue, New York, NY 10010
An imprint of Greenwood Publishing Group, Inc.

Printed in the United States of America

∞

The paper used in this book complies with the Permanent
Paper Standard issued by the National Information Standards
Organization (Z39.48—1984).

10 9 8 7 6 5 4 3 2 1

To
Milton and Yvonne Fife, my parents.
Thanks for your love, support, and guidance.

Contents

Illustrations

FIGURE

TABLES

Acknowledgments

The writing of this book was made possible with the generous assistance of many people. The contributions of Eduard Ziegenhagen and Michael McDonald were especially numerous and valuable. They helped to refine both the theoretical and methodological aspects of this work, and encouraged me to challenge prevailing assumptions in this field.

A large debt of gratitude is owed to Christine Rossell for her generous provision of data. Indeed, she truly made this time-series analysis possible, for I was unable to obtain data for some of the years relying upon my own resources. The reader would benefit by examining her perspectives on this issue, most notably in *The Carrot or the Stick for School Desegregation Policy: Magnet Schools or Forced Busing?* Our conclusions may differ, but she provided me with many new ideas about desegregation in the first place.

I would be remiss if I did not extend my gratitude to the administrators in the twenty school districts studied in the book. Their cooperation in the provision of data and substantive information about their desegregation plans was enthusiastic and very much appreciated. The Office for Civil Rights (OCR) in the Department of Education was also most helpful. Further thanks go to the Kentucky, New York, Oregon, Texas, and Wisconsin state education departments.

This book was greatly enhanced by the contributions made by many fine people. Any errors that exist, however, are solely my responsibility.

The greatest thing happened to me during the course of researching and writing this book. I met, fell in love with, and married a wonderful woman. I am very fortunate to have you, Melissa. You have enriched my life tremendously and I look forward to walking down the path of life with you. It is and will be an exciting adventure.

DESEGREGATION
IN AMERICAN
SCHOOLS

Chapter 1

School Desegregation Since Brown I

STATEMENT OF THE PROBLEM: THE NEED FOR A NEW ANALYTICAL FRAMEWORK

Researchers have attempted to analyze the relative effectiveness (the reduction of the level of segregation) of various types of school desegregation interventions to determine which type aids the process of racial desegregation in the American public schools best. Questions have been raised about the best strategies of compliance for desegregation purposes. Disputes regarding whether mandatory or voluntary school desegregation plans most successfully achieve this goal continue. Yet few conceptual distinctions discerning mandatory from voluntary school desegregation plans have been incorporated in previous research designs (e.g., Rossell, 1990a, 1990b, 1988, 1979; Rossell & Clarke, 1987; Smylie, 1983; Morgan & England, 1982; and Royster, Baltzell, & Simmons, 1979). A voluntary plan for desegregation to one researcher may be considered as a mandatory one by another.

With this in mind, the main thrust of this research effort is to construct an analytical framework to distinguish among, and to ascertain the relative impact of, the intervention strategies identified. The concern here is with facilitating the reduction of the level of segregation, a primary objective of desegregation. The investigation is about the effectiveness of alternative strategies in school desegregation policy, and not about the merit of desegregation itself. The impact of desegregation on learning and social behavior is another question. Thus, the central research question is, *Which type of school desegregation intervention facilitates the reduction of the level of segregation in the public schools best?*

The ensuing discussion is a summary of the major court cases dealing with the school desegregation issue. The analysis contains a substantive interpretation of the judicial decisions, and does not address the implementation issue in depth as this facet will be examined in Chapter 4.

SCHOOL DESEGREGATION SINCE *BROWN I*: LANDMARK CASES AND THE EVOLUTION OF TECHNIQUES[1]

Many questions regarding the constitutionality of various school desegregation techniques have been resolved by the federal judiciary. The issue of school desegregation became a prime focus of the nation's public policy debate in 1954, when the highest tribunal concluded that "in the field of public education the doctrine of 'separate but equal' has no place. Separate educational facilities are inherently unequal."[2] The Court reversed the "separate but equal" doctrine that it had announced in 1896.[3] Legal (*de jure*) segregation,[4] whether permitted or required, was deemed to violate the equal protection of the laws guaranteed by the Fourteenth Amendment. Chief Justice Warren reasoned that "to separate them from others of similar age and qualifications solely because of their race generates a feeling of inferiority as to their status in the community that may affect their hearts and minds in a way unlikely ever to be undone."[5]

Even though the physical facilities or other tangible factors may be equal, the Supreme Court ruled that the separation of the races deprived the minority children of equal educational opportunities. Since the Court deemed that "education is perhaps the most important function of state and local governments,"[6] these entities were no longer constitutionally allowed to permit the legal segregation of the races to continue.

The Court provided implementation guidelines for *Brown I* a year later, in *Brown II*.[7] School districts were directed to make a prompt and reasonable start toward full compliance with the *Brown I* desegregation mandate; the burden rested upon them to demonstrate that additional time was necessary in the public interest to comply. Additional time, however, must be consistent with good-faith compliance at the earliest practicable date. During the period of transition from segregated to desegregated schools, federal district courts would oversee the progress to this end. Chief Justice Warren directed that this was to occur "with all deliberate speed."

Brown I made it imperative to dismantle dual school systems. An early method adopted to supposedly accomplish this was a "freedom of choice" plan (Welch & Light, 1987: 29). The Supreme Court, however, virtually ended the use of freedom of choice plans in 1968, in *Green v. County School Board of New Kent County, Virginia*.[8] At the time of this case, New Kent County was a rural county in eastern Virginia with a population of approximately 4,500. Half of the population was black. *De facto* segregation (segregation by the fact of where people live) was not present, because people of both races resided throughout the county. The school system only had two schools. Approximately 1,300 pupils went to these schools, 740 blacks and 550 whites. The New Kent school on the east side of the county was a white combined elementary and high school; the George W. Watkins school was a black combined elementary and high school located on the west side. The freedom of choice plan in the district·was in operation for three years. No white children during this time chose to attend the Watkins school; 115 black children enrolled in the New Kent school in 1967, yet 85 percent of the black children remained in the Watkins school.[9]

Justice Brennan, speaking for a unanimous Court, declared:

We do not hold that "freedom of choice" can have no place in such a plan. We do not hold that a "freedom-of-choice" plan might of itself be unconstitutional, although that argument has been urged upon us. Rather, all we decide today is that in desegregating a dual system a plan utilizing "freedom of choice" is not an end in itself....If the means prove effective, it is acceptable, but if it fails to undo segregation, other means must be used to achieve this end.[10]

The Court ruled that these types of plans did not aid the process of desegregation, and declared that other types of methods must be utilized to comply with *Brown I*. In studying various desegregation techniques, it is always important to remember Justice Brennan's words:

There is no universal answer to complex problems of desegregation; there is obviously no one plan that will do the job in every case. The matter must be assessed in light of the circumstances present and the options available in each instance.[11]

Swann v. Charlotte-Mecklenberg Board of Education (1971)[12] dealt with several varying desegregation techniques. The North Carolina school district involved had more than 84,000 pupils in the 1968–69 school year. Seventy-one percent of them were white and 29 percent were black (about 24,000 students). Twenty-one thousand of these students attended schools within the city of Charlotte. Of these, 14,000 black children attended schools that were at least 99 percent black. In 1965, a federal district court approved a desegregation plan based upon geographic zoning with a free transfer provision. Swann petitioned for further relief in 1968, based on *Green v. County School Board of New Kent County, Virginia*. The school board and a court-appointed expert, Dr. John Finger, both submitted plans for approval.[13]

The school board plan called for the closing of seven schools and the reassignment of the students involved. The board restructured school attendance zones to achieve greater racial balance, but kept the existing grade structures intact. Pairing and clustering techniques for desegregation were rejected; the free transfer plan was modified into an optional majority to minority (M to M) transfer system. The racial basis of the school bus system was to be abolished, and the plan would racially mix the faculty and administrative staff. With respect to high schools, blacks were to be reassigned to nine of the ten high schools in the district, thereby producing 17–36 percent black population in each. The tenth high school, Independence, was projected to have a 2 percent black attendance rate. Junior high schools would be rezoned so that twenty schools would range from 0 to 38 percent in black attendance. The other junior high school was located in a black neighborhood and would still have a black enrollment of 90 percent. The elementary schools, however, would rely entirely upon gerrymandering of geographic zones. Over half of the black children of elementary school age would remain in nine schools that were between 86 and 100 percent black.

The Finger plan adopted the school board's zoning plan for high schools with one modification—an additional 300 black students would be transported to the nearly all-white Independence High School. This plan employed much of the rezoning plan of the board for junior high schools, but also created nine "satellite" zones. A satellite zone is an area that is not contiguous with the main attendance zone surrounding the school. Under this proposal, inner-city black students were to be assigned by attendance zones to nine outlying predominantly white junior high schools. The significant point of departure came with respect to elementary schools. Rather than simply relying on geographic zoning, Finger proposed the utilization of zoning, pairing, and grouping techniques, with the result that all elementary schools would range from 9 to 38 percent black.[14]

The district court accepted a modified version of the school board's plan dealing with the faculty and for secondary schools in the district. It adopted Finger's plan for elementary schools. As a whole, the court's approved plan was essentially the Finger plan. This plan called for more desegregation than the school board was willing to accept. On appeal to the United States Circuit

Court of Appeals, the part of the district court's order relating to the faculty and secondary schools was affirmed, but the order relating to the elementary schools was vacated because it would place an unreasonable burden on the students and the school board.[15] A unanimous Supreme Court affirmed the district court's decision, in favor of the Finger plan. Chief Justice Burger asserted that "the objective today remains to eliminate from the public schools all vestiges of state-imposed segregation."[16] Burger admitted that, by 1968, very little progress had been made in the elimination of dual school systems, even though the *Brown I* decree had been handed down fourteen years earlier. The *Swann* case was especially troublesome for the Court because it dealt with several desegregation issues.

The central issue of *Swann* was that of student assignment. The Supreme Court addressed four "problem areas." The Fourteenth Amendment Equal Protection Clause permitted federal courts to decree as tools of desegregation in de jure racially segregated school systems

1. reasonable bus transportation;
2. reasonable grouping of noncontiguous school zones;
3. reasonable movement toward the elimination of one-race schools; and
4. the use of mathematical ratios of blacks and whites in the schools as a starting point in the process of racial desegregation.

The first major Supreme Court decision involving schools outside the South was *Keyes v. School District No.1, Denver, Colorado* (1973). In 1969, there were 96,580 students in the Denver school system. During this year, the school board adopted three resolutions—1520, 1524, and 1531—designed to desegregate the schools in the Park Hill area in the northeast section of the city. Following a school board election, the resolutions were rescinded and a voluntary student transfer program was established. Keyes then requested an injunction against the rescission of the resolutions. The district court found that the school board had engaged in an unconstitutional policy of deliberate racial segregation with respect to the Park Hill schools. It ordered the board to desegregate the schools involved by implementing the three resolutions. Segregation, however, was not simply a problem in the Park Hill area, so Keyes petitioned the court to desegregate all of the segregated schools in Denver. The court concluded that the rest of the school district was not segregated by law or action, but that there was de facto segregation. Thus, the court deemed it could not order a desegregation remedy to achieve better racial balance. Yet at the very least, the court did acknowledge that the segregated core of schools in the city of Denver were educationally inferior to the predominantly white schools, so the school board was required to provide "equal educational opportunity." It decreed a varied remedial plan to achieve desegregation and thus "equal educational opportunity" in these schools. Upon appeal, the Tenth Circuit Court of Appeals affirmed the decree with respect to the Park Hill schools. It reversed the ruling regarding the core city schools, however.[17]

Speaking for the majority of the Court, Justice Brennan ruled that official action leading to de facto segregation must be remedied in the same manner as de jure segregation (Welch & Light, 1987: 29). Brennan explained:

> We emphasize that the differentiation factor between *de jure* segregation and so-called *de facto* segregation to which we referred in *Swann* is purpose or intent to segregate. Where school authorities have been found to have practiced purposeful segregation in part of a school system, they may be expected to oppose system-wide desegregation, as did the respondents in this case, on the ground that their purposefully segregative actions were isolated and individual events, thus leaving plaintiffs with the burden of proving otherwise. But at that point where an intentionally segregative policy is practiced in a meaningful or significant segment of a school system, as in this case, the school authorities cannot be heard to argue that plaintiffs have proved only "isolated and individual" unlawfully segregative actions.[18]

This case is also significant because it extended the desegregation remedy to include Hispanic students as well as blacks.

Milliken v. Bradley (1974) was an extremely divisive case that was decided by a 5 to 4 split vote. Bradley and other black students along with the Detroit branch of the National Association for the Advancement of Colored People (NAACP) brought a class action suit against Michigan Governor William Milliken, the State Board of Education, Detroit's school board and superintendent, and other state officials, alleging racial segregation in the Detroit public schools. The federal district court ruled for Bradley and the other black students. It ordered the school board to formulate desegregation plans for the city school system and ordered state officials to devise plans for a unitary system of education for the three-county metropolitan area. The court also allowed eighty-five surrounding school districts to participate in the case even though they were not found to have violated the Fourteenth Amendment Equal Protection Clause. The court appointed a panel to devise a regional plan including the Detroit system and fifty-three of the eighty-five suburban districts. It also ordered the Detroit school board to purchase 295 school buses for the purpose of busing. The court of appeals affirmed the district court's ruling but remanded the case for more extensive participation by the affected suburbs and tentatively rescinded the order to the Detroit board concerning the immediate purchase of buses.[19]

The Supreme Court reversed these lower decisions. Chief Justice Burger declared that both courts acted on the erroneous assumption that the Detroit schools could not be truly desegregated unless the racial composition of each school reflected the racial composition of the entire metropolitan area. The record, according to Burger, only demonstrated evidence of de jure segregation in Detroit:

> With no showing of significant violation by the 53 outlying school districts and no evidence of any interdistrict violation or effect, the court went beyond the original theory of the case as framed

by the pleadings and mandated a metropolitan area remedy. To approve the remedy ordered by the court would impose on the outlying districts, not shown to have committed any constitutional violation, a wholly impermissible remedy based on a standard not hinted at in *Brown I* and *II* or any holding of this Court.[20]

Thus, the Court ruled that the Fourteenth Amendment Equal Protection Clause did not mandate the creation of a regional school district composed of a central city in which de jure segregation is present and suburban school districts where the record does not indicate segregation in order to establish a better racial balance for the metropolitan area.[21]

A year after *Milliken v. Bradley*, in *Newburg Area Council, Inc. v. Board of Education of Jefferson County*, the United States Court of Appeals for the Sixth Circuit ruled that the stringent conditions set out in *Milliken* were met.[22] It ordered the first interdistrict remedy for the Louisville and Jefferson County, Kentucky school districts. That same year magnet schools were sanctioned as components of a desegregation plan in Boston.[23] Magnet schools were established as part of a court-ordered mandatory plan to desegregate the Boston public schools.[24]

SUMMARY

The judicial branch of government has addressed the question of viable techniques for desegregation in compliance with *Brown I*. Major decisions regarding techniques were rendered prior to the mid-1970s. The *Milliken* decision has been the central focus of many school desegregation analysts as it has limited desegregation efforts to central city districts where de jure segregation has been practiced. Many argue that metropolitan remedies are essential due to white migratory practices to the suburbs. Despite the judicial rulings on techniques, there is still no consensus in the literature as to whether a mandatory or voluntary strategy reduces segregation in the schools best. Included in Chapter 2 is a discussion of the various mandatory and voluntary techniques for desegregating school districts. The issue of measuring segregation is also addressed.

NOTES

1. The definition of desegregation utilized here is borrowed from Leronia Josey (Ed.), *Desegregation Resource Handbook.* (Philadelphia: Philadelphia School District, Office of Community Affairs. 1974). ERIC Document ED 103 500:

> *Desegregation*: [The], complex social and political process of reassigning pupils and teachers in order to end racial or ethnic isolation in the public schools....The most complete desegregation is generally said to exist when the racial balance in each school matches the racial composition of the total school community (p. 18).

The reader is reminded that the focus of this evaluation is on desegregation itself, and not on integration. Integration entails the uniting of differing races or ethnic groups as one—an ideal that cannot be achieved without desegregating schools first.

2. *Brown v. Board of Education of Topeka, Kansas (Brown I)*, 347 U.S. 483, 98 L.Ed. 873, 74 S. Ct. 686 (1954).

3. *Plessy v. Ferguson*, 163 U.S. 537, 41 L.Ed. 256, 16 S. Ct. 1138 (1896).

4. Josey (1974, pp. 17–18) provides a distinction between de jure and de facto segregation:

> *De jure segregation*: de jure segregation in fact refers to any separation of students by race which results from official school board, city or state action.

> *De facto segregation*: a separation of students by race which the law recognizes as having happened either by sheer accident or because of housing patterns, with no local or state action responsible for the separation.

5. *Brown v. Board of Education of Topeka, Kansas (Brown I)* 347 U.S. 483, 98 L.Ed. 873, 74 S. Ct. 686 (1954).

6. Ibid.

7. *Brown v. Board of Education of Topeka, Kansas (Brown II)*, 349 U.S. 294, 99 L.Ed. 1083, 75 S. Ct. 753 (1955).

8. *Green v. County School Board of New Kent County, Virginia*, 391 U.S. 430, 20 L.Ed. 2d 716, 88 S. Ct. 1689 (1968).

9. Ibid.

10. Ibid.

11. Ibid.

12. 402 U.S. 1, 28 L.Ed. 2d 554, 91 S. Ct. 1267 (1971).

13. Ibid.

14. Ibid.

15. Ibid.

16. Ibid.

17. *Keyes v. School District No.1, Denver, Colorado*, 413 U.S. 189, 37 L. Ed. 2d 548, 93 S. Ct. 2686 (1973).

18. Ibid.

19. *Milliken v. Bradley*, 418 U.S. 717, 41 L.Ed. 2d 1069, 94 S. Ct. 3112 (1974).

20. Ibid.

21. For a detailed analysis of *Milliken*, see Conference Before the United States Commission on Civil Rights, *Milliken v. Bradley: The Implications for Metropolitan Desegregation* (Washington, D.C.: U.S. Government Printing Office, November 9, 1974).

22. *Newburg Area Council, Inc. v. Board of Education of Jefferson County*, 521 F.2d 578 (6th Cir. 1975).

23. *Morgan v. Kerrigan*, 401 F. Supp. 216 (D. Mass. 1975).

24. For a more in-depth analysis of the Louisville/Jefferson County and Boston desegregation plans, see Chapter 3.

Chapter 2

Mandatory Versus Voluntary School Desegregation Strategies

Ascertaining the effectiveness of public policy interventions is one critical component of evaluation studies. At times this is difficult because of flaws in conceptualization and measurement strategies in the evaluation process. A noteworthy illustration of this is in the school desegregation literature, where an ongoing debate continues to focus on strategies for facilitating the reduction of racial imbalance, a primary objective of desegregation. One method by which this is done involves allowing parents to have some input as to where their children attend school, thus implying a situation of voluntary school desegregation. When parental input is virtually nonexistent and no element of choice is involved, a mandatory school desegregation plan is said to be in effect. This is slightly misleading, however, because parents may choose to leave the district altogether to avoid desegregation efforts, or they may enroll their children in private schools. The question remains: Do elements of choice provided by the local school district enhance the desegregation of public schools, or are more coercive means necessary to facilitate the reduction of segregation? A discussion of the primary desegregation techniques assists in understanding what is commonly referred to as "mandatory" and "voluntary."

ASSESSING SCHOOL DESEGREGATION TECHNIQUES

There are three primary voluntary desegregation techniques, and three that could be classified as involuntary or mandatory (Rossell & Clarke, 1987: 4–5). The primary voluntary techniques are open enrollment (sometimes referred to as freedom of choice), majority to minority transfers, and magnet schools. Open enrollment allows students to transfer to any school within their district. A student cannot be denied his or her choice unless the school's maximum capacity has been exceeded. This technique is rarely used any longer in and of itself because it can be a means by which white students leave schools that are becoming desegregated.

M to M transfers are utilized to a much greater extent and permit any student to voluntarily transfer from a school where he or she is in the majority to a school where he or she is in the minority. Student participation is greatest among older blacks; white students rarely volunteer. There is greater participation, however, of all groups if transportation is provided.

Magnet schools have been successful in motivating white students to attend formerly minority schools. Magnet schools are schools with a special curriculum or teaching style designed to attract students of differing racial and ethnic backgrounds to a desegregated setting. Many districts with an M to M program do not have magnets, but it is rare to find a magnet school plan without an M to M program (Rossell & Clarke, 1987: 4).

The primary mandatory techniques include pairing and clustering, rezoning, and magnet schools. In pairing, two schools (one minority and one white) are combined by either sending half the students in one school to the other for all grades or by sending all the children to one school for certain grades and then to the other school for the rest of the grades. The latter is by far more common. For example, a predominantly white school and predominantly black school both offer grades K–6. These schools become paired by converting one into a lower elementary school (grades 1–3) and the other into an upper elementary school (grades 4–6). Kindergarten would be unaffected by the plan. The grouped schools may have either contiguous or noncontiguous attendance zones (Welch & Light, 1987: 27). Clustering is simply the same technique for more than two schools.

Rezoning occurs when attendance areas are redrawn so that nearby schools will become more desegregated. This type of strategy varies tremendously in its scope—it may affect only two schools or may alter the attendance zone of every school in the district. Rezoning can occur in a variety of ways. Contiguous rezoning alters the attendance boundaries between adjacent schools. Noncontiguous rezoning reassigns students to schools that do not share a boundary with their present schools. Noncontiguous rezoning usually entails greater transportation costs (Welch & Light, 1987: 26–27).

Lastly, magnet schools can be a part of a coercive plan (such as Boston) and cannot be considered a voluntary technique as such. The purpose of magnets in such plans is to reduce the "white flight" and hostility that are presumed to result from desegregation efforts and not to provide degrees of choice (Rossell & Clarke, 1987: 5).

Desegregation plans may include predominantly mandatory techniques, voluntary techniques, or a combination of the two. Nonetheless, research efforts to date have relied on the traditional mandatory-voluntary dichotomy when school desegregation plans are operationalized. These studies have generated mixed results.

Several empirical studies exist comparing the relative effectiveness of school desegregation plans for reducing the level of segregation in the public schools (e.g., Rossell, 1990a, 1990b, 1988, 1979; Rossell & Clarke, 1987; Welch & Light, 1987; Smylie, 1983; Morgan & England, 1982; and Royster, Baltzell, & Simmons, 1979). In general, the majority of studies until very recently (Christine Rossell's recent research efforts) have determined that mandatory plans are more successful at reducing segregation.

Rossell's work can be viewed as a significant departure from the scholarship on school desegregation to date. She has determined that voluntary plans with incentives (magnets) are more effective than mandatory reassignment plans at reducing segregation in urban America. Rather than measuring segregation as racial balance, Rossell assesses segregation levels by utilizing an interracial exposure index. Understanding the differences between these two measures may aid in the voluntary versus mandated school desegregation debate.

MEASURING SEGREGATION: THE INDEX OF DISSIMILARITY VERSUS THE INTERRACIAL EXPOSURE INDEX

Many research efforts have focused on finding the most reliable measure of school desegregation (e.g., James & Taeuber, 1985; Kelly & Miller, 1989; Rossell & Clarke, 1987; Rossell, 1985a; Clotfelter, 1978; Zoloth, 1976; and Giles, 1974). The most recent debate centers on the plausibility and viability of the two most common indexes used to measure segregation—the Index of Dissimilarity (D) (also known as the Taeuber Index) and the Interracial Exposure Index (Smw).

No consensus has emerged in the desegregation literature regarding the preferred measure for segregation. Different studies employ different measures, with little or no justification or discussion. James and Taeuber (1985: 2) offer an explanation for this problem:

> One reason for the disagreement is the absence of a clear set of criteria, derived from a comprehensive definition of segregation, which can be used to evaluate the various measures that have been proposed. In the absence of such criteria, analysts have been forced to rely upon convenient interpretations of certain measures to justify their use. Choosing a measure of segregation on the basis of one's attraction to a certain interpretation introduces a degree of arbitrariness into the index selection procedure because there

is often no clear reason to prefer one index over another, especially since many measures have several interpretations. A more serious problem is the tendency to use the measure that is currently popular, thereby allowing the definition of segregation to flow from one's choice of a measure rather than the reverse.

Further distinction, therefore, is warranted to distinguish D from *Smw*.

The Index of Dissimilarity

The Index of Dissimilarity is a measure of racial balance and was originally created to measure progress toward housing desegregation (see Taeuber & Taeuber, 1965: 195–254). The formula for this is

$$D = \left[\frac{1}{2} \sum \left| \frac{b_i}{b_t} - \frac{w_i}{w_t} \right| \right] \times 100,$$

where

b_i = the number of black students in school i
b_t = the total number of black students in the district
w_i = the number of white students in school i
w_t = the total number of white students in the district

D is equal to one-half the sum of the absolute value of the number of blacks in each school divided by the total number of blacks in the district minus the number of whites in each school divided by the total number of whites in the district, multiplied by 100. By multiplying by 100, this standardized statistic falls between 0 and 100.

The index represents the percentage of black students who would have to be reassigned to white schools, if no whites are reassigned, in order to have the same proportion of blacks in each school as in the entire district. Zero indicates perfect racial balance, meaning that no black students need to be reassigned and that the racial proportion in each school is the same as in the district as a whole. A score of 100 indicates perfect racial imbalance; all of the black students need to be reassigned, if no whites are reassigned, in order to achieve perfect racial balance. A situation of perfect racial imbalance would be indicative of a dual school system—all schools are uniracial.

The Interracial Exposure Index

The Interracial Exposure Index (*Smw*) is a measure of the interracial exposure of minorities to whites. The formula for this is

$$Smw = \sum kN_{km}P_{kw} / \sum kN_{km},$$

where

k = each individual school

N_{km} = number (N) of minorities (m) in a particular school (k)

P_{kw} = proportion (P) white (w) in the same school (k)

Smw is equal to the proportion of white students in the average minority child's school. The number of minority students in each school is multiplied by the proportion of white students in the same school. This number is summed for all schools and divided by the number of minority students in the school system to produce a weighted average—the proportion white in the average minority child's school. The index is therefore a measure of the percentage of white students that minority children are exposed to in their school. Unlike D, it is an unstandardized mean-based statistic. The lowest score a district can generate utilizing this measure is 0, meaning that minority children are not exposed to any nonminority (white) children. The upper limit depends on the percentage of whites in the school district. For example, if a school district is 40 percent white, a score of .40 indicates perfect interracial exposure between minorities and whites.

Segregation: A Measure of Dispersion

James and Taeuber (1985) determine that segregation refers to the degree of dispersion between the races, most commonly between black and white. Under this conception, segregation pertains to heterogeneity across a district's schools in the proportion of black students. It is the differential distribution of blacks and whites. The purpose of any segregation index is to gauge the magnitude of that differential. The spatial unit to which the index is applied is the school district and its corresponding subunits (schools within the district)—the same unit utilized in this study and all others attempting to compare various school desegregation interventions.

An underlying theme suggested by James and Taeuber (1985) is that measures of segregation, and therefore dispersion, are all variations on the same theme—that of the Gini Index. The formula for G is

$$G = \sum_i \sum_j t_i t_j \left| p_i - p_j \right| / 2T^2 P(1 - P),$$

where

T = total population size

P = proportion of one component group (e.g., blacks)

t_i = total population of school i

p_i = proportion of one component group (e.g., blacks) in school i

The numerator is the weighted mean of the absolute values of all possible differences between schools in the proportion who are black. The denominator equals the maximum possible value for the numerator (which occurs when all students are in uniracial schools) given the black proportion P of the district (James & Taeuber, 1985: 5). G varies between 0 and 1—0 indicating no segregation and 1 indicating completely segregated conditions (this could be modified by multiplying by 100 to set the scale at 0 to 100).

Measures of Central Tendency

Measures of central tendency refer to interracial exposure or contact between the races. Exposure indexes describe the average racial composition encountered by students of a particular race. This differs from James and Taeuber's (1985) conception of segregation, which examines the differences in the distribution of social groups (e.g., blacks and whites) in a particular spatial unit (e.g., school districts, cities, neighborhoods). Thus, segregation indexes quantify the deviation of a set of schools from a baseline of no segregation. This is not the case with exposure indexes, as they reflect weighted averages, for example, the proportion of white students in the average minority child's school. Such measures attempt to capture two dimensions with a single indicator. Like segregation indexes, exposure indexes seek to capture the racial mixing of students. Yet at the same time, measures of central tendency do not hold changing population demographics constant. Instead, these measures attempt to reflect a second dimension—that of the mixing of students without losing them to assumed "white flight." Thus, measures of dispersion are reflective of racial balance, while measures of central tendency attempt to measure racial balance and "white flight" with a single indicator.

James and Taeuber (1985: 4) compare and contrast these differing measures:

There is an association between segregation and interracial exposure. Completely segregated schools prevent any within-school interracial contact whereas completely integrated districts produce maximum exposure. Between these two extremes, the association is loose. In fact, the goal of increasing interracial contact within a school district may conflict with the goal of desegregation. Similarly, enrollment shifts that change segregation dramatically need not have a pronounced effect on interracial exposure.

Given the conception of segregation discussed above and its unidimensional nature, it would seem that interracial exposure indexes "are better regarded as compositional rather than distributional measures" (James & Taeuber, 1985: 4). These indexes do not measure what they purport to—they do not adequately capture racial balance, like segregation indexes, and are premised on the assumption that whites will "flee" desegregation orders. This may be overly simplistic, as decreases in white enrollment in urban public schools may be due to other factors, such as economic prosperity and a declining birth rate.

D: A Viable Measure of Segregation

As a statistical measure, *D* is both valid and reliable. It measures exactly what it purports to measure. From a policy perspective, Kelly and Miller (1989) determine that *D* carries a policy bias, however. They maintain that *D* does not measure the actual level of exposure of black students to white students (Kelly & Miller, 1989: 432–34). Indeed, this is not *D*'s purpose. *D* is designed to capture exclusively the phenomenon of segregation. Thus, to argue that *D* does not capture the level of interracial exposure goes beyond the realm of dispersion and into the dimension of exposure, which is a different concept. Kelly and Miller (1989) also determine that evaluators favoring *D* would put "the user's emphasis on eliminating schools that are unrepresentative of the total district in their individual racial composition" (p. 432). This may be a strong assertion, since desegregation relies on the reassignment of students. They further explain that, "in districts which have a majority of ethnic minority students, every school would have to have a numeric minority of whites in order to approach the 0 Taeuber score. Those who might rely exclusively on the Taeuber Index would likely be proponents of this even-distribution style of desegregation" (pp. 432–33). Bear in mind, however, that this may be an oversimplification of *D* enthusiasts, in that many analysts of school desegregation are highly critical of the restrictions set forth by the Supreme Court in *Milliken*. With the national trend of white migration to the suburbs over the past few decades, many researchers believe that the focus of urban school desegregation should be on the metropolitan regions as a whole and not simply on the inner city.

Smw: A Nonviable Measure of Segregation

Rossell and Clarke (1987) conclude that, "if the instrumental goal of school desegregation is to bring whites and minorities into contact with each other, then the best measure of that is interracial exposure rather than racial balance. Racial balance is an inadequate goal because it ignores how many whites are coming into contact with minorities" (p. 15). Yet *Smw* is not a viable measure of segregation in the first place. It is simply a measure of central tendency.

Rossell (1990a, 1990b, 1988, 1985), and Rossell and Clarke (1987) have produced, according to Kelly and Miller (1989), "policy-biased, hypothetical examples of how the Interracial Exposure Index measures reality" (p. 434). Table 2.1 shows one of these examples and includes contrived data for a hypothetical school system with six schools. Two possible outcomes are also suggested. Rossell and Clarke (1987) conclude that Outcome A should be preferred over Outcome B, because 44.2 percent of whites are in the average minority child's school (*Smw* = .442), and only 2 percent of the whites in Outcome A are in the average minority child's school (*Smw* = .020). This conclusion is reached, despite the fact that Outcome B is perfectly racially balanced (*D* = 0) and Outcome A is more racially imbalanced than Outcome B (*D* = 8.8).

Rossell attributes the drastic decline in white students to anticipated "white flight," which may indeed be a distortion of reality. Considering that this example assumes 98 percent white

Table 2.1
Hypothetical School System A with Six Schools

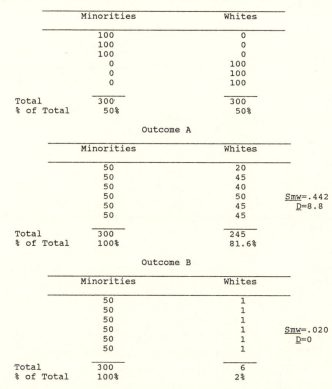

	Minorities	Whites	
	100	0	
	100	0	
	100	0	
	0	100	
	0	100	
	0	100	
Total	300	300	
% of Total	50%	50%	

Outcome A

	Minorities	Whites	
	50	20	
	50	45	
	50	40	
	50	50	$Smw=.442$
	50	45	$D=8.8$
	50	45	
Total	300	245	
% of Total	100%	81.6%	

Outcome B

	Minorities	Whites	
	50	1	
	50	1	
	50	1	
	50	1	$Smw=.020$
	50	1	$D=0$
	50	1	
Total	300	6	
% of Total	100%	2%	

Sources: Rossell (1990a:478; 1990b:35; 1988:327; 1985:220); Rossell & Clarke (1987:16); Kelly & Miller (1989:434).

enrollment loss during the first year of implementation, this is probably not a harsh criticism. Consider the following illustration.

White Enrollment Losses in Boston

Controversy abounded during Boston's desegregation process. Extensive white enrollment losses due to desegregation were

Table 2.2

Minority and White Enrollment in the Boston Public Schools, 1967/68–1988/89

Year	Minority%	White%	Change in White % From T-1 to T	
1967	27.3	72.7	----	
1968	31.5	68.5	-4.2	
1969	34.0	66.0	-2.5	
1970	35.9	64.1	-1.9	
1971	38.5	61.5	-2.6	
1972	40.4	59.6	-1.9	
1973	42.8	57.2	-2.4	
1974	47.6	52.4	-4.8	[Phase I]
1975	52.9	47.1	-5.3	[Phase II]
1976	56.0	44.0	-3.1	
1977	58.4	41.6	-2.4	
1978	60.4	39.6	-2.0	
1979	62.9	37.1	-2.5	
1980	64.8	35.2	-1.9	
1981	67.7	32.3	-2.9	
1982	70.2	29.8	-2.5	
1983	72.1	27.9	-1.9	
1984	72.3	27.7	- .2	
1985	72.6	27.4	- .3	
1986	74.1	25.9	-1.5	
1987	75.5	24.5	-1.4	
1988	76.7	23.3	-1.2	

feared. Table 2.2 includes the proportions of white and minority enrollment in the Boston public schools from the academic years 1967/68–1988/89. The data reflect white enrollment losses for every year during this period. The greatest losses occurred during the two primary years of implementation, 1974–75 and 1975–76 (Phases I and II, respectively). Yet these losses amounted to 4.8 percent and 5.3 percent of the total enrollment, respectively. There is a great difference between the concrete illustration of Boston and the 98 percent loss in Rossell's (1990a, 1990b, 1988, 1985) and Rossell & Clarke's (1987) example.

D or *Smw*?: One Best Measure

From a theoretical perspective, social scientists who seek to measure the phenomenon of segregation would be wise to utilize

D, because it measures racial balance. *Smw* attempts to capture two phenomena with a single indicator, which is both theoretically and statistically suspect. *D*, however, at least measures the concept desired. Kelly and Miller (1989) conclude that "no single measure of desegregation is adequate to interpret how a school district has progressed on its path to racial integration" (p. 437).

Yet researchers concerned about assessing desegregation efforts, such as Kelly and Miller, should differentiate segregation from interracial exposure in the first place. Therefore, evaluators interested in addressing desegregation are quite clearly urged to use *D*. Kelly and Miller's own analysis of the Index of Dissimilarity should have rendered a different conclusion.

Chapter 3

Twenty Districts: From Boston to Tulsa

A descriptive analysis of the desegregation plans implemented in each of the twenty school districts in this study is provided in this chapter. Information sources for similar research are very scattered and in some cases rather scant. When courts are involved one can obtain published opinions—unpublished or unreported opinions may also be available. Local and national newspapers often contain pertinent information. Some school districts maintain continuous records documenting their desegregation efforts. Others do not, especially when the plans date back in time. Information may also be centralized at the state or national level—various state education departments keep records on desegregation in the local districts. At the federal level, the Office for Civil Rights has published monographs on many local desegregation efforts nationwide. Interviewing local officials may also be enlightening. Finally, published articles, monographs, and books are obviously helpful, as is ERIC, the Education Resources Information Center.

A brief historical background is provided for each of the districts; these descriptions are not intended to be in-depth case studies. Several issues are covered for each district: desegregation techniques, implementation years, racial composition goals (if any), and the sources of the desegregation plans. Population figures for each city are listed at the beginning of each section, utilizing

1940, 1950, 1960, 1970, and 1980 census data.[1] A summary is included at the end of the chapter, and a new classification scheme for measuring the relative impact of school desegregation interventions follows. Reviewing the discussion on differing desegregation techniques in Chapter 2 may prove helpful.

BOSTON, MASSACHUSETTS (BOSTON PUBLIC SCHOOLS)

City Population

1940	770,816
1950	801,444
1960	697,197
1970	641,071
1980	562,994

Because of the intense conflict and media attention involved, the fact that the national focus switched from the South to the supposedly liberal enclave of Boston, and for a host of other reasons, volumes of accounts on school desegregation in the Boston public schools have been documented.[2] On one hand, the city maintained a progressive intellectual tradition through its cultural and academic institutions. Yet at the same time, Boston's neighborhoods had a history of being clearly delineated by race and ethnicity.

Movement toward desegregating the public schools began in 1961, when the district adopted an open enrollment policy. Its intent was to provide a means by which black students could transfer to predominantly white schools. As the United States Commission on Civil Rights reported, "For over a decade this policy remained in effect. It achieved nothing as far as school integration was concerned, since white students were also free to transfer from schools whose compositions were not to their liking" (1975: xiv–xv). In April 1965, a report by the Massachusetts Advisory Committee to the Massachusetts commissioner of education determined that forty-five schools were racially imbalanced—that is, more than 50 percent nonwhite (United States Commission on Civil Rights, 1975: xv). According to the committee, open enrollment alone could not properly desegregate the schools (United States Commission on Civil Rights, 1975: xv).

These findings, coupled with increased pressure from the black community in Massachusetts, led to the passage of the Racial Imbalance Act of 1965. The act stipulated that any school with a nonwhite enrollment of more than 50 percent was imbalanced. The commissioner of education could refuse to certify all state school aid to localities that did not comply (United States Commission on Civil Rights, 1975: xv).

Although this act included the most progressive school desegregation requirements in the country, the Commission on Civil Rights declared that it did little to desegregate the Boston public schools (1975: xv). It did not require the desegregation of all-white schools, prohibited involuntary interdistrict transportation, and had vague guidelines for determining compliance. This resulted in procrastination by the Boston School Committee. The eight years following passage of the act were dominated by conflict between the state education authorities and the Boston School Committee. The litigation battle commenced in the Massachusetts state courts (United States Commission on Civil Rights, 1975: xv–xvi).

Because progress toward desegregation was less than expeditious, black parents organized their own programs to help achieve equal educational opportunities for their children. Roxbury residents created Operation Exodus to transport almost six hundred black students to predominantly white schools during the 1965–66 school year. In the fall of 1966, blacks organized the Metropolitan Council for Educational Opportunity (METCO), which was another transfer program that transported black students to suburban school districts that volunteered to take them (United States Commission on Civil Rights, 1975: xvi).

On November 15, 1971, Judge Robert Sullivan of the Suffolk Superior Court entered a preliminary injunction enjoining the

State Board of Education from withholding state funds from the
Boston School Committee.[3] The Board of Education had done so
because it determined that the Boston public schools had not made
reasonable progress in eliminating racial imbalance under the
Racial Imbalance Act of 1965. The board wanted the court to
order the School Committee to file a plan to eliminate racial
imbalance; the withholding of state funds would continue until
such a plan was filed and implemented.[4] On February 2, 1973,
the Superior Court, through Judge Reardon, affirmed the judge's
decree:

> There was no error in the judge's finding and in the ruling based
> thereon, the board acted "arbitrarily, in abuse of its discretion,
> and in a manner not consistent with the public interest."[5]

On October 29, 1973, the Massachusetts Supreme Judicial
Court approved a desegregation plan by the State Board of
Education for the Boston public schools.[6] The Board of Education
had previously rejected a Short Range Plan Toward Elimination
of Racial Imbalance in the Boston Public Schools 1972–73,
submitted by the School Committee in November, 1972.[7] This
plan was designed to meet the limited requirements of the Racial
Imbalance Act. It proposed to reduce the number of imbalanced
schools from sixty-one to forty-two by redistricting and reorganizing the grade structure into elementary (K–5), middle (6–8),
and high schools (9–12) (United States Commission on Civil
Rights, 1975: xvii). The Board of Education adopted its own plan
as a recommendation to the School Committee. On February 15,
1973, the Supreme Judicial Court remanded the case to the Board
of Education to hold hearings and develop an administrative
record so that proper judicial review of the board plan and the
committee plan could ensue.[8] Hearings were held between March
20 and May 3, 1973. On May 29, 1973, the hearing examiner
submitted his Report and Recommendations to the Board of
Education. Upon receiving written objections to the report, the
examiner issued an Opinion and Order on June 25, 1975. This

reaffirmed the board's earlier rejection of the committee plan and called for implementation of the revised board plan in the fall of 1974.[9] The approved board plan called for redistricting of schools but also took cognizance of the limitations imposed by the neighborhood district requirement. Elementary school districts would have a maximum length of two miles and intermediate school districts would have a maximum length of five miles.[10]

To make matters even more complex, the NAACP filed suit in March 1972 in federal district court, alleging that action by the School Committee had created and maintained a segregated school system. Furthermore, in November 1971, the Department of Health, Education, and Welfare (HEW) wrote a letter to the School Committee charging discrimination in certain educational programs. Two years later, HEW threatened to cut off all federal education funds to the district (United States Commission on Civil Rights, 1975: xvi–xvii).

The federal suit of *Morgan v. Hennigan* was decided on June 21, 1974, in the U.S. District Court for the District of Massachusetts.[11] Plaintiffs in the case included black parents and their children. The defendants included the Boston School Committee, its individual members, the superintendent of the Boston public schools, the Board of Education of the Commonwealth of Massachusetts, its individual members, and the Massachusetts commissioner of education. Judge W. Arthur Garrity, Jr., wrote the opinion of this well-known case:

> The court has looked for and weighed valid, nondiscriminatory justifications for the defendants' decisions and actions. Only when there were none or when there was clear evidence of discriminatory purpose, has the court found that the defendants' intent was segregative.[12]

In this decision, Garrity made several rulings. First, the court found that school authorities had knowingly carried out a systematic program of segregation, which affected all of Boston's students, teachers, and school facilities, and had thereby created and maintained a dual school system. Second, Judge Garrity held that the entire school system was unconstitutionally segregated in violation of the Fourteenth Amendment Equal Protection Clause. Further, the court ruled that the Massachusetts Board of Education and its commissioner of education were not responsible for the maintenance of a dual system, but would be retained as parties for the purposes of remedial relief. The Boston School Committee was permanently enjoined from discriminating on the basis of race in the operation of the Boston public schools, and the court ordered that implementation of the plan approved by the Massachusetts Supreme Judicial Court should proceed as scheduled, in September 1974. The district was further ordered to begin the formulation and implementation of plans that would eliminate all forms of racial segregation in the Boston public schools.[13]

Garrity's decision was affirmed by the First Circuit Court of Appeals on December 19, 1974.[14] Chief Judge Coffin quoted Supreme Court Justice Felix Frankfurter:

> Deep emotions have . . . been stirred. They will not be calmed by letting violence loose . . . submitting to it under whatever guise employed. Only the constructive use of time will achieve what an advanced civilization demands and the Constitution confirms.[15]

The techniques utilized to stimulate desegregation during Phase I (1974–75) included the redrawing of district boundaries and pairing of schools; magnets were added a year later (Welch & Light, 1987: 87).

Judge Garrity issued the plans for Phase II (1975–76)[16] on May 10, 1975.[17] The city was divided into eight neighborhood school districts and one citywide district. The reassignment of students into the eight districts was done by geocodes. A geocode is a bounded area of between five and fifteen residential blocks. The geocodes used in Boston were originally developed as reporting units for use by the Boston Police Department.[18] The citywide school district established twenty-two magnet schools that were paired with area colleges, businesses, and cultural institutions.[19] The racial composition goals of the plan were to have each school in the eight neighborhood districts reflect the overall racial composition of that subdistrict, plus or minus 25 percent (Rossell & Clarke, 1987: 24). On appeal, the First Circuit upheld all aspects of the Phase II plan on January 14, 1976.[20]

On May 3, 1976, Judge Garrity issued his Phase IIB order for implementation in 1976–77. This order included no new educational programs or district changes; the basic emphasis was on the refinement of the plan already in effect (Bullard, Grant, & Stoia, 1981: 57). The Phase III order was issued on May 6, 1977, and implemented in the 1977–78 school year. Garrity directed the establishment of a permanent agency, the Department of Implementaton (DI) within the school system to administer and monitor every phase of the desegregation order (Dentler, 1978: 75). At the same time, he ordered compliance with a previous requirement that all kindergartens be desegregated wherever possible (Cohen, 1977: 9).

In 1977, the district court directed the School Committee, the city of Boston, and the State Board of Education to submit a Unified Facilities Plan (UFP).[21] The plan was to include a schedule for school closings, construction and renovation, and repair and refurbishing for all nine school districts through 1986.[22] Six months later the group submitted a UFP that was subsequently rejected by the district court. The Citywide Parents Advisory Council (CPAC) found the plan

> to be based upon inaccurate and insufficient data; to ignore educational, desegregation, and community factors in the decision; to burden minority children unfairly in its pattern of school closings; to fail to prove its economic arguments for closing; to overlook the long-term implications for Boston of its recommended actions.[23]

On March 21, 1978, the district court rejected the proposed revision of the UFP. In response, a Manual for District Planning Activities was submitted on April 23, 1979. The manual contained a six-step planning process and included criteria for determining future school closings. The court approved the manual on August 15, 1979.[24] At the same time, however, the court determined that some parts of the manual "imply erroneously that safeguarding continuity and stability of the education process is of equal importance to achieving desegregation and equal education opportunity."[25] It ordered the reformulation of a new UFP that: "shall eliminate by July 1, 1980 no fewer than half of all excess seats (as of April 15, 1979) in elementary schools; and shall identify by name elementary school facilities to which students will not be assigned for the 1980–81 school year."[26]

On October 3, 1979, a new draft of the UFP was submitted, and became known as the "Green Book."[27] It called for the immediate closing of sixteen elementary schools. On November 29, 1979, Boston School Superintendent Wood sent a memorandum to the School Committee in which he recommended revisions to the UFP. In what became known as the "Wood Plan," the number of elementary schools scheduled for closing was reduced to ten.[28] This plan also proposed two new categories of facilities—"linkage" and "beacon" schools.[29] These two categories would be utilized instead of designating the schools as "support" schools.

Under the linkage proposal, contiguous community district elementary schools were to be paired for assignment purposes. Under the beacon proposal, students could apply for a limited number of seats in selected elementary schools ("beacon" schools) in their district as an alternative to attending their regularly assigned school. Such assignments could be made only if they enhanced desegregation at the beacon school and did not put the regularly assigned school out of compliance with the Phase II racial quotas.[30] Both proposals were rejected by the district court and affirmed by the First Circuit.[31]

On September 3, 1985, Garrity approved of a new UFP that outlined several renovation projects in the district.[32] In his Final

Orders decree, Garrity determined that the Boston school system could either maintain the racial composition requirements of the Phase II order, or, beginning with the 1986–87 year or thereafter, use a single citywide guideline for assigning students. Enrollments at every school (except District 8 schools) would be arranged so that they would fall within a range of .25 times the percentage of each racial group and be based upon the citywide public school population of K–12 as of April 1 of the previous year, minus bilingual and special students.[33] The requirement of adherence to the mathematical ratios of Phase II was later vacated by the First Circuit, which determined that the constitutional violation had been remedied and that unitary status had been achieved by the district.[34]

Desegregation in Boston is still an ongoing controversy. On February 27, 1989, the Boston School Committee, dividing along racial lines, voted 9–4 to adopt a new student assignment plan (Wen, February 29, 1989: 1,12). Mayor Raymond Flynn was a primary catalyst in creating the plan. Under the new plan, Boston would be divided into three geographical zones and parents would choose schools for their children within their zone. Schools of choice would be provided as long as assignments did not cause overcrowding or disrupt the school's racial balance. All schools would reflect the racial composition of the zone as a whole. The blacks on the committee believed that the new plan would resegregate the city's schools. The issue of implementation will likely be determined by the courts once again.

BUFFALO, NEW YORK (BUFFALO PUBLIC SCHOOLS)

City Population

1940	575,901
1950	580,132
1960	532,759

1970   462,768
1980   357,870

On April 30, 1976, Chief Judge John T. Curtin of the U.S. District Court, Western District of New York, ordered the Buffalo public schools to desegregate.[35] Plaintiffs included black and white parents of public school children in the Buffalo metropolitan area, the Citizens Council for Human Relations, Inc., and the Buffalo branch of the NAACP. They argued that actions and inactions by the school board caused the school system to become or remain extremely segregated. Among the major allegations were segregation of staff, siting and construction of schools so as to promote segregation, manipulation of school district lines, and the creation of optional zones and transfers for segregative purposes.[36] As a result of these actions, the plaintiffs claimed that they were being denied the equal protection of the laws guaranteed by the Fourteenth Amendment.

The defendants in this case can be categorized into two groups. The state defendants included Ewald Nyquist, the New York commissioner of education, and the Board of Regents of New York and its individual members. The city defendants included Joseph Manch, the superintendent of schools of the city of Buffalo at the time the suit was brought, Eugene Reville, the present superintendent, the Board of Education of the city of Buffalo and its members, the Common Council of the city of Buffalo and its members, and Stanley M. Makowski, mayor of the city of Buffalo. The defendants admitted that many of the schools were racially imbalanced. Yet they maintained that any imbalances were due to demographic shifts in housing patterns and not by school board activity. In other words, they argued that the schools were de facto segregated and not de jure segregated.[37] Judge Curtin adhered:

> The court finds, therefore, that the defense of residential segregation, like the "racially neutral" neighborhood school policy defense to which it is intimately related, is essentially a smokescreen. Furthermore, the court finds that the city

defendants' past action and inaction which have, to a substantial degree, caused, exacerbated or maintained the segregated housing conditions, are separate and independent alternative grounds for holding them constitutionally liable for the segregated condition of the schools in Buffalo.[38]

In subsequent litigation, the U.S. Court of Appeals for the Second Circuit held that Curtin's ruling enjoining the defendants from taking any further action in violation of the plaintiffs' constitutional rights and ordering implementation of certain sections of the board's desegregation plan and submission of further plans were both appealable.[39] The defendants asked the district court to reconsider its decision in light of recent Supreme Court decisions, but Curtin reaffirmed his earlier liability decision.[40] In a case focusing more closely on the individuals involved, the court of appeals affirmed the district court's reaffirmation with regard to the city officials, but reversed it with regard to the state officials.[41]

Judge Curtin has continuously acted as the overseer of implementation of desegregation in Buffalo. Phase I was approved by Curtin on July 9, 1976, and implemented in the fall of 1976 (Buffalo Public Schools, n.d.: 1). Among the steps taken were continuation of the Quality Integrated Education program (an M to M program), open enrollment, and alternative high schools. Segregated schools were closed and magnet schools were created (Buffalo Public Schools, 1976: 4). The racial composition goals were to make each school have a minority enrollment between 30 and 65 percent (Rossell & Clarke, 1987: 23). Phase II of the Buffalo Plan was approved by the court on May 4, 1977 and implemented in the fall of 1977 (Buffalo Public Schools, n.d.: 1). Phase III was approved by the court on June 19, 1980 and implemented that fall (Buffalo Public Schools, n.d.: 2). On January 13, 1981 Judge Curtin ordered desegregation to be expedited (Buffalo Public Schools, n.d.: 2). Phase IIIx was approved on May 19, 1981, and implemented that fall (Buffalo Public Schools, n.d.: 2–3).

This involved the elimination of all middle schools and pairing of twenty schools.

CINCINNATI, OHIO (CINCINNATI PUBLIC SCHOOLS)

City Population

1940	455,610
1950	503,998
1960	502,550
1970	452,524
1980	385,457

A desegregation suit was first filed against the Cincinnati Board of Education in 1963 by the NAACP on behalf of Tina Deal, a student in the city schools. The board won in the U.S. District Court, and the U.S. Court of Appeals for the Sixth Circuit affirmed that judgment (Griffin, 1977: 87). On remand in 1969, the district court determined "that neither gerrymandering nor any other alleged discriminatory practice on the part of the board brought about such racial imbalance as existed" (Griffin, 1977: 87). The board was cleared of all claims of constitutional deprivation by the district court and all of the findings were affirmed by the court of appeals (Griffin, 1977: 87).

On June 29, 1970, the board declared its support for neighborhood schools and outlined its goal of "better intercultural understanding":

It will be the goals of the Cincinnati Board of Education to provide interracial and intersocioeconomic educational understanding for both the students and the teachers of the Cincinnati Public School system thereby giving the students and the teachers a more realistic knowledge of the multicultural nature of our society. Recognizing that provincialism contributes to misunderstanding among groups separated by geography as well as other factors, the schools must devise methods for regular dialogue among representatives of different areas, bringing differences and even conflicting views into open discussion and examination.

Ohio law requires the equal opportunity for every child to attend the most convenient school regardless of race, creed or national origin. With this in mind, the Board of Education supports the neighborhood school concept. Nothing in the goal set forth in this Section F shall conflict with the legal requirements of convenience nor require the voluntary or involuntary ansportation of students (Griffin, 1977: 88).

On July 9, 1973, the superintendent discussed implementation of these goals. New teachers would be assigned to schools on the basis of their training and certification, as well as their race. The intent would be to have the racial balance of each school staff approach the racial composition of the entire school system within plus or minus 10 percent. Several years would be allowed to realize this goal. An open enrollment plan would also be implemented in the fall of 1973. The conditions for this program would depend on the availability of space at the receiving school as well as the improvement of racial balance. Following this announcement, the board drew up an application for funds under the Emergency School Assistance Act (ESAA) in the summer of 1973. The funds were to be used to assist in the desegregation of one high school district. The regional office of the U.S. Department of Health, Education, and Welfare verbally informed the board that it was making sufficient efforts to warrant the application (Griffin, 1977: 89).

Litigation soon resurfaced after a lame duck Board of Education passed a resolution to abolish the district lines and assign students so that each school would resemble the racial balance of the district as a whole. The new board, however, focused its efforts on continuation of the neighborhood school policy. In response, HEW reduced the allowable amount of funds that the district could receive under the ESAA application (Griffin, 1977: 89).

As a result of this action by the HEW office for Region Five, the school board sought relief in the U.S. District Court for the

Southern District of Ohio.[42] Judge David S. Porter ruled that the court had jurisdiction over the suit under its federal question jurisdiction; that the secretary of HEW did not abuse his discretion in approving the various regulations involved in the case; and that the decisions made by the officials of HEW in denying the district's application for emergency desegregation funds were not arbitrary, capricious, or abusive. The judge stated that the mere possibility that the district might apply again for such funding and again be denied funds for failure to implement a previously adopted plan or an alternative plan equally promising in the judgment of HEW did not present the court with a situation of sufficient urgency to warrant the declaratory relief sought by the district. On March 31, 1976, the U.S. Court of Appeals, Sixth Circuit, reversed the judgment of the district court.[43]

In a case[44] reflecting principles similar to those of the original suit filed in 1963, the court of appeals ruled that the plaintiffs could not go beyond July 26, 1965, in their attempt to prove violation of the Fourteenth Amendment:

> In its opinion the district court held that the question of segregative intent was critical to the decisions in *Deal I* and *II* and that this issue was settled by a finding that the Cincinnati Board had no such intent up to July 26, 1965, when the *Deal* inquiry ended. Thus, the court held that the inquiry in the present case is limited to the existence of segregative intent in the period since July 26, 1965.[45]

Circuit Judge Lively affirmed the earlier ruling, maintaining that the plaintiffs had failed to demonstrate that actions or inactions by the school board had resulted in racial segregation in the schools.

The ten-year ongoing litigation battle of *Bronson v. Board of Education of the City School District of Cincinnati* was settled on June 22, 1984.[46] In a settlement agreement, the school district agreed to continue reducing racial isolation by the continuation and expansion of alternative schools supported by state funds.

The plaintiffs agreed that the case, if it went to trial, would be long and expensive, so a settlement was deemed fair and in the public interest.

The major desegregation plan for the Cincinnati public schools was phased in from 1973-74 through 1976-77. It included magnet schools, majority to minority transfers, and rezoning (Welch & Light, 1987: 88). More alternative schools were created in September 1977, 1980, 1981, 1983, 1984, 1985, and 1986 (Cincinnati Public Schools, 1985: 6-7). No numerical goals were established (Rossell & Clarke, 1987: 23).

DALLAS, TEXAS (DALLAS INDEPENDENT SCHOOL DISTRICT)

City Population

1940	294,734
1950	434,462
1960	679,684
1970	844,401
1980	904,078

Desegregation in the Dallas Independent School District (DISD) has been the subject of an ongoing court battle since 1955.[47] A number of black children were denied admission to white schools and brought suit against the district. They sought a declaratory judgment and injunction requiring the district to cease its practice of segregating students on the basis of color (Jung, 1988: 1).

The original suit was dismissed by a federal district court because it determined that the suit was premature and that the DISD should have a chance to complete a series of studies on the effects of desegregation (Jung, 1988: 1-2). The Fifth Circuit Court of Appeals reversed this ruling in 1956 and remanded the case to the district court for a retrial. Following the new hearing, the district court once again dismissed the case. On appeal, the

Fifth Circuit reversed and directed the DISD to desegregate "with all deliberate speed." Following this ruling, the district court ordered the DISD to cease racial segregation, effective as of the midwinter 1957–58 school term. This time, the Fifth Circuit determined that the district court was proceeding too quickly, and it reversed the order—the DISD was given the opportunity to formulate a desegregation plan before deadlines were imposed by a federal court (Jung, 1988: 2).

On April 16, 1958, the district court entered an order requiring the DISD to desegregate "with all deliberate speed." The Texas Constitution, however, still required "separate but equal" schools. Furthermore, the Texas state legislature had also passed a law making it a misdemeanor to abolish a dual school system without a public referendum called by a petition of 20 percent of the voters. State funds would be cut off for those districts that actually did so. Another law made it illegal to assign children to desegregated schools if their parents objected in writing. (These laws were not repealed until 1969) (Jung, 1988: 3). The district unsuccessfully sued the state commissioner of education, seeking clarity between conflicting state and federal obligations (Jung, 1988: 3).

By May 1959, no desegregation plan had been formulated so the initial plaintiffs sought an order requiring desegregation by September 1960. The relief was denied, but the district was ordered to file a desegregation plan by May 1960. The district complied, and a plan calling for a twelve-year "stairstep" desegregation program beginning in the fall of 1961 was presented. The district court subsequently rejected the plan and opted for a freedom of choice plan. This plan would keep the dual school system, but also provide for desegregated schools as well. The Fifth Circuit reversed this ruling and ordered the district court to implement the "stairstep" plan (Jung, 1988: 3–4).

Implementation of this plan began in September of 1961. Yet only eighteen black first graders entered eight formerly all-white elementary schools (Dallas Independent School District, n.d.b: 3). In September 1962, the plan included second graders. A total of twenty-eight black students attended white schools (Dallas Independent School District, n.d.b: 3). Third graders were included in 1963, to increase the total number of black students attending white schools to 182 (Dallas Independent School District, n.d.b: 3). Fourth graders were included in the plan in 1964. In 1965 the Fifth Circuit dismantled the "stairstep" plan and ordered the district court to review a school board plan that called for desegregation of the elementary schools in the fall of 1965, the junior high schools in the fall of 1966, and the senior high schools in the fall of 1967 (Dallas Independent School District, n.d.b: 4). During the same year, single attendance zones for all elementary schools were established, and black twelfth graders were allowed to enroll in previously all-white schools. Dual attendance zones were eliminated for junior and senior high schools in 1966 and 1967, respectively. Formally, de jure segregation was abolished at this time (Jung, 1988: 4), thirteen years after *Brown I*.

On October 6, 1970, twenty-one black and Hispanic students filed a new desegregation suit against the DISD. This case contended that segregation had been maintained "through choice of building sites, staffing of administrative offices, and teaching positions, and through the use of the neighborhood assignment plan" (Dallas Independent School District, n.d.b: 5).

On July 16, 1971, District Judge William M. Taylor, Jr., of the Northern District of Texas, Dallas Division, ruled that the racial composition of seventy schools in the district indicated that elements of a dual school system still remained. The district was ordered to implement a desegregation plan that would utilize, among other things, television in the schools to establish audio and visual contact and communication among the students.[48] Nevertheless, Taylor held "that the Board of Education of DISD is in good faith and is committed to the principle of equal quality education."[49] In a supplemental decision on August 2, 1971, Taylor entered the first comprehensive desegregation order for the DISD.[50] Implementation of the plan began in the fall of 1971, utilizing magnet schools, majority to minority transfers, grade reorganization, the redrawing of attendance zones, and pairing and clustering (Rossell & Clarke, 1987: 27). Racial composition goals were to make grades four through eight between 25 and 75 percent minority (Rossell & Clarke, 1987: 24).

With respect to Taylor's "TV plan" for elementary schools, classrooms containing students of different races would spend at least one hour per day in a two-way television communication with one another; at least one weekly, three-hour direct visit would also occur between the paired classrooms. At the secondary level, Taylor ordered busing of over fifteen thousand junior and senior high school students. One week later this portion of the order was altered, and the court approved of DISD's proposal for busing seven thousand students instead.[51]

The Fifth Circuit stayed Taylor's order concerning the "TV plan" until an appeal could be heard. This did not occur for almost four years (Jung, 1988: 6). Finally, on July 23, 1975, the Fifth Circuit rejected the "TV plan," as well as the busing plan for secondary schools, as inadequate.[52] Circuit Judge Simpson said this of the "TV plan":

It is undisputed that the "television plan" would not have altered the racial characteristics of the schools operated by the DISD. The Supreme Court has made it clear that nothing less than the elimination of predominantly one-race schools is constitutionally required in the disestablishment of a dual school system based upon segregation of the races. For this reason, the district court's elementary school "television plan" must be rejected as a legitimate technique for the conversion of the DISD from a dual to a unitary educational system.[53]

Simpson also criticized the district's secondary school plan:

The objective of reducing the proportionate share of a racial group's composition of the student population of a particular school to just below the 90% mark is short of the Supreme Court's standard of conversion from a dual to a unitary system. The 90% figure adverted by the plaintiffs in this case was clearly utilized only for purposes of emphasis; it was never intended by the plaintiffs to represent the magic level below which a school would no longer be categorized as "one race." The DISD's approach to the problem of desegregation of its secondary schools fails to indicate a bona fide effort to comply with the mandates of the Supreme Court. The district court's plan for the desegregation of the DISD's secondary schools must be rejected as constitutionally inadequate.[54]

Thus, the 1971 plan was dismantled and the case was remanded to the district court to establish a new desegregation plan.

When the case returned to the district court, the plaintiffs sought to add seven suburban districts to the case and thus require an areawide desegregation plan. They eventually dropped six of these districts but kept the Highland Park Independent School District. On December 11, 1975, the district court ruled against the plaintiffs.[55] Taylor maintained that the plaintiffs had failed to demonstrate that the Highland Park district had caused any segregative effect on the Dallas ISD. This decision was later affirmed by the Fifth Circuit.[56]

A new desegregation plan was approved by the district court on March 10, 1976.[57] The plan was fairly complex and included these elements among others:

1. Majority to minority transfers.
2. The DISD would be divided into six subdistricts. Four were to reflect the overall ethnic composition of the DISD, plus or minus 5 percent (Northeast, Northwest, Southeast, and Southwest). Seagoville and East Oak Cliff would be exempt from this requirement.
3. Grade levels would be standardized:

   K–3 = elementary schools

   4–6 = intermediate schools

   7–8 = middle schools

   9–12 = high schools

4. Seventeen thousand students in grades 4–8 would be sent to desegregated intermediate and middle schools centrally located in their district. A desegregated school was defined as a school with a minority ratio within plus or minus 10 percent of the subdistrict's ratio.

5. Students in grades 9–12 would be assigned to the high school in their regular attendance zones.

6. More magnet schools would be created.[58]

Implementation commenced in 1976–77 and continued through 1980–81 (Dallas Independent School District, n.d.b: 8).

The litigation battle did not end here, however. On February 1, 1982, District Judge Barefoot Sanders entered a judgment that established a new desegregation plan for the DISD.[59] This 1982 plan built upon the 1976 plan and basically was a continuation of the same techniques with some alterations. The district was reorganized into three new subdistricts based on feeder attendance zones to high schools.[60] Implementation of the plan commenced in 1982–83 (Welch & Light, 1987: 90).

On April 30, 1984, the district court permitted the school district to amend the desegregation plan and establish one-race remedial centers for certain minority students who were diagnosed as having reading deficiencies. Some schools were excluded from this program.[61] The amended portion of the 1982 plan was implemented in 1984–85 (Welch & Light, 1987: 90). The Fifth Circuit later affirmed the lower court ruling on September 20, 1985.[62] In effect, the plan created three educational centers for grades four through six in South Dallas (Jung, 1988: 14).

On February 3, 1986, the district court approved the creation of four West Dallas centers for remedial education for students in grades four through six. Students from six West Dallas attendance zones were to attend these centers instead of their North Dallas schools.[63] These West Dallas centers opened in the fall of 1986 (Jung, 1988: 15).

DAYTON, OHIO (DAYTON PUBLIC SCHOOLS)

City Population

1940	210,718
1950	243,872
1960	262,332
1970	243,601
1980	203,371

Physical segregation of the Dayton public schools into separate buildings of students and teachers by race was ruled illegal in Ohio in 1926.[64] After *Brown I*, in 1956, the Ohio attorney general ruled that the Ohio State Board of Education had the primary responsibility for administering the laws relating to the distribution of state and federal funds to local school districts. Such funds could not be distributed to local districts that segregated students on the basis of race in violation of *Brown I*. Despite protests over a twenty-year period by the Dayton branch of the NAACP and others, the district still operated the majority of its schools on a strictly racial basis. The State Board of Education allowed this to happen without upsetting the flow of state and federal money to Dayton. On March 17, 1969, the Office for Civil Rights of the Department of Health, Education, and Welfare notified the district that it was not complying with Title VI of the Civil Rights Act of 1964—blacks were not afforded the same educational opportunity as whites. On June 7, 1971, the Ohio State Department of Education presented a series of recommendations to Dayton, which included a sharp criticism of the board's policy that effectively segregated the middle schools in the district. Dayton did not comply with all of the state's recommendations, yet continued to receive funding from the State Board of Education.[65]

The Dayton school board appointed a committee to evaluate and advise the board on plans to reduce racial isolation and improve educational opportunities on April 29, 1971. On December 8, 1971, the board passed three resolutions that would have initiated district-wide desegregation by the fall of 1972. Yet by January 3, 1972, new board members took office as a result of the November 1971 election. The three resolutions were rescinded, meaning that the system's Freedom of Enrollment program and existing attendance zones were reinstated. As a result, black and white parents brought suit against the district.[66]

The complaint was filed in the United States District Court for the Southern District of Ohio, Eastern Division, which is located in Columbus (the Western Division is located in Dayton). This court found three constitutional violations of the Fourteenth Amendment Equal Protection Clause: (1) racially imbalanced schools, (2) optional attendance zones, and (3) the school board's rescission of the three resolutions. The United States Court of Appeals for the Sixth Circuit affirmed this holding of a cumulative violation of the Fourteenth Amendment.

The lower court ordered the Dayton school board to present it with a desegregation plan to remedy these constitutional violations. The local board complied, and submitted an eleven-point plan called the "free choice plan." Other plans were submitted by the three-member minority of the Dayton school board and the Dayton Classroom Teachers' Association. The court of appeals, however, ruled that this plan could not remedy the existing violations and remanded the case to the district court with orders to revise its order dealing with the desegregation plan.[67]

When called upon to review the constitutionality of the case for a second time, Chief Judge Phillips of the Sixth Circuit Court of Appeals noted that, although the term de jure did not appear in the first decision, the meaning of the decision was that the Dayton school system was guilty of unlawful segregation practices. On remand, the district court was directed to adopt a systemwide desegregation plan to be implemented in the 1976–77 school year that would conform to the Supreme Court's decisions in *Keyes* and *Swann*.[68] The district complied, and implementation commenced in the fall of 1976 as ordered. Techniques included the redrawing of attendance zones, pairing and clustering, grade reorganization, and magnet schools (Rossell & Clarke, 1987: 27).

On July 26, 1976, the court of appeals affirmed the district court's order requiring that each school's ratio of black to white students be within plus or minus 15 percent of the racial makeup of the system. According to the higher court, the use of mathematical ratios did not violate the Supreme Court's rulings, and the district court did not misconceive the constitutional requirements for a unitary system. The court of appeals found that the plan did not violate the Supreme Court rule proscribing requirements of annual adjustments in attendance zones to prevent the development of racially segregated schools within unitary systems if the changes in the racial mix were caused by factors for which the school authorities could not be considered responsible.[69]

The court of appeals' decision was appealed to the United States Supreme Court by the Dayton Board of Education. A unanimous Court (Justice Marshall did not participate) vacated the district court's judgment and remanded the case. The majority, through Justice Rehnquist, maintained that the constitutional violations did not justify the broad districtwide remedy imposed, and that the district court must formulate more specific findings and, if necessary, gather more evidence. Rehnquist summized that the court of appeals did not reverse any findings of fact by the district court nor engage in any fact-finding of its own. Given the three violations cited by the lower tribunal and affirmed by the court of appeals, the Supreme Court ruled that the imposition of a systemwide remedy of pairing, redefinition of attendance zones, and a variety of special programs and magnet schools was not warranted to overcome the constitutional violations present in the Dayton school system.[70]

On remand from the Supreme Court, the district court located in the Western Division (Dayton) dismissed the plaintiffs' complaint for basically five reasons:

1. Acts of intentional segregation that ended over twenty years ago were not constitutional violations in the absence of the showing of incremental segregative effects.

2. The policy of establishing and maintaining neighborhood schools was not in and of itself a constitutional violation.

3. The Board of Education's rescission of action was not in and of itself a constitutional violation.

4. The racial imbalance in the school system was not in and of itself a constitutional violation.

5. The plaintiffs failed to prove both segregative intent and incremental segregative effect required to establish violation of the Fourteenth Amendment Equal Protection Clause.[71]

On appeal, the court of appeals held that the constitutional violations found in Dayton had a systemwide impact. Accordingly, it ordered the district court to reinstate the desegregation plan that was approved in the previous court appearance. The case was once again remanded to the district court.[72]

On certiorari for the second time, the Supreme Court affirmed the court of appeals' approval of systemwide desegregation in *Dayton II*.[73] This time, the Court was split 5–4 (White, Brennan, Marshall, Blackmun, and Stevens comprised the majority). Justice White, writing for the majority, held that the Dayton district was operating a dual school system in violation of the Equal Protection Clause. He also noted that the court of appeals committed no prejudicial errors of fact or law.

DES MOINES, IOWA (DES MOINES INDEPENDENT COMMUNITY SCHOOL DISTRICT)

City Population

1940	159,819
1950	177,965
1960	208,982
1970	200,587
1980	191,003

A Special Committee on Equal Educational Opportunity was established on August 1, 1967, to study methods by which the Des Moines Independent Community School District could change its policies to expedite desegregation. After eleven months of study, the committee determined that equal educational opportunity did not exist for all students. The committee recommended that action be taken to end de facto segregation. To accomplish this, the committee suggested implementation of a pilot program in Logan school, which was more than 90 percent black. In the fall of 1968, twenty-eight minority students were transported to other schools and twelve nonminority students were brought to Logan. Nash school later participated in this program, which was called the voluntary transfer program (Des Moines Public Schools, n.d.: 4). From the 1974–75 until the 1984–85 school year, students were allowed to enter the voluntary transfer program at any time during their elementary years, at the beginning of transitional school, or at the beginning of high school. The policy was changed in the fall of 1985, when students were required to enroll in the program before sixth grade in order to participate (Des Moines Public Schools, n.d.: 6).

An open enrollment policy for all grades was adopted by the school board on April 4, 1972. Enrollment was open to students in the home attendance area first, and then to students in other areas. This was modified in the spring of 1985–any student in the Harding or North attendance areas must attend those schools. Exceptions were made for those in the voluntary transfer program (Des Moines Public Schools, n.d.: 10–11).

Despite these initial policy responses to segregation in the Des Moines public schools, the district received a letter on April 4, 1973, from the Iowa Department of Public Instruction, notifying it that a condition of minority group isolation existed. The district was cited for noncompliance with the state guidelines on nondiscrimination in Iowa schools. The state superintendent requested that the district submit a report to the Department of Public Instruction Urban Education Section, detailing direct action by the board to eliminate racial isolation in the schools. The school board complied, and the Department of Instruction in turn declared that the voluntary transfer and open enrollment programs had little, if any, effect upon the growing racial isolation in Des Moines. It requested that the school system develop and submit a plan to eliminate segregation. The first draft was to be prepared within 120 days, and the deadline for the final plan was June 15, 1975 (Des Moines Public Schools, n.d.: 12–13).

The board approved a plan on January 22, 1974, and presented it to the state on February 15, 1974. The eight-point plan proposed by the district was accepted on March 15, 1974. A City-Wide Advisory Committee on Intercultural Affairs met to make recommendations to the board for desegregating the Des Moines schools. Later that year, on November 20, 1974, the Office for Civil Rights of the Department of Health, Education, and Welfare[74] conducted an on-site review of the district's activities. Its purpose was to determine the presence or absence of racial segregation. A final report by the steering committee of the City-Wide Advisory Committee was presented to the school board on January 21, 1975, and on June 19, 1975, the board submitted a revised desegregation plan to the Department of Public Instruction (Des Moines Public Schools, n.d.: 14–16). It was clear that the voluntary transfer program had failed to substantially reduce minority isolation, as the vast majority of students participating in the program were black. Magnet schools also were unable to attract significant participation by whites. The district rejected the state's proposal that the minority enrollment ceiling in any single school be lowered from the existing level of 50 percent to 32 percent. (The total minority enrollment in 1976–77 was 13 percent.)

In the interim, the district received a letter of noncompliance from OCR on September 20, 1976. Analysis of historical data led OCR to believe that conditions of segregation had not occurred without full awareness, consent, and support of the school board. The following is a summary of its findings:

1. Elementary attendance zones from 1960 to 1976 were drawn to have the effect of assigning minority children to schools that were virtually all-minority in enrollment.

2. Certain schools sharing a common boundary but distinctly different in racial makeup were continuously overcrowded, while others were underutilized.

3. Optional attendance areas appeared to have no purpose other than to allow continued racial segregation of students. They were established between schools with high concentrations of minorities and schools that were virtually all nonminority.

4. The district took actions in support of the continued segregation of students in the selection of sites for new school construction, the building of additions on overcrowded nonminority schools that shared a common boundary with underutilized schools with concentrations of minority students, and the closing of minority schools and unlikely reassignment of these schools.

5. Teacher and principal assignments at the elementary and junior high levels paralleled the segregation of students, and made it possible to identify racially disproportionate schools by reference to the racial composition of their facilities.

6. A substantial number of national origin minorities were excluded from effective participation in the educational program offered by the district. The identification of students needing services was cited as being inadequate, and bilingual notices and letters were not used to communicate with parents whose home or primary language was not English (Des Moines Public Schools, n.d.: 21–23).

The board sought to comply with OCR's findings through a Memorandum of Understanding dated November 16, 1976. It had thirty days to submit a corrective plan to eliminate racial discrimination.

Implementation of the board's plan ensued in the fall of 1977. The effort was basically threefold:

1. Restructuring elementary student assignments.

    a. Merging two attendance areas (pairing) and thus develop-
ing three two-center schools (Cassady/Monroe, Ed-
munds/Jefferson, and King/Perkins).

    b. Merging three attendance areas (clustering) and thus de-
veloping a three-center school (Findley/Oak Park/Moul-
ton).

    c. Closing one school (Logan) and merging the attendance
area with an adjacent school (Garton).

  2. Establishing a bilingual center.

  3. Continuing the voluntary transfer program.

School closings also occurred in 1979, 1981, and 1983. In the
fall of 1984, Edmunds/Jefferson was de-paired, as Edmunds
became a magnet school and Jefferson became a receiving school
for the voluntary transfer program (Des Moines Public Schools,
n.d.: 23–27).

HOUSTON, TEXAS (HOUSTON INDEPENDENT SCHOOL DISTRICT)

City Population

1940	384,514
1950	596,163
1960	938,219
1970	1,232,802
1980	1,595,138

School desegregation began in the Houston Independent
School District (HISD) in the fall of 1960, when it implemented
a grade-per-year transfer plan (Cunningham, 1978: 1). This was
in response to a suit filed in 1956 to eliminate the dual school
system in the HISD. As Trombley (1977a: 92) explained: "The
initial response from school trustees was 'the usual Southern
rigmarole,' a school spokesman said. 'You know—first, it was
never, then it was one grade a year.'" This plan was deemed

ineffective in terms of desegregating the HISD, and gave way to a freedom of choice plan that was initially implemented in the fall of 1967 (Cunningham, 1978: 1).

The HISD was found to be operating a dual school system on May 30, 1970, by Chief Judge Ben Connally of the U.S. District Court for the Southern District of Texas, Houston Division.[75] He ordered the district to implement an equidistant school zoning plan for all levels of instruction. This involved drawing equidistant zone lines between adjacent schools, with students required to attend the school nearest their home except for those participating in the majority to minority transfer program. On appeal, the Fifth Circuit Court of Appeals modified the equidistant zoning plan by ordering a geographical capacity plan for the secondary schools and the pairing, clustering, and rezoning of twenty-five elementary schools.[76] On September 18, 1970, Connally entered an Amended Decree, which is still in operation in the HISD today.[77] This plan provides for majority to minority transfers, the redrawing of attendance zones, and pairing, and was first implemented during the 1970–71 school year.[78]

Soon after implementation of this plan, a group of citizens living in the middle western section of the HISD began organizing an independent school district designated the Westheimer Independent School District (WISD). This area contained approximately eight thousand students who were almost 90 percent white. The State Board of Education approved its creation, but Chief Judge Connally enjoined the district's creation on April 4, 1973:[79]

It is with considerable reluctance that I find it necessary . . . to restrain the proponents from following prescribed statutory procedures for the creation, for their own purposes, of a new government agency. The action is taken because in my judgment it will seriously impede the further efforts of the H.I.S.D. and of this Court to create a completely unitary system, and because I believe it would constitute a very dangerous precedent.[80]

In an Injunction Decree dated April 30, 1973, Connally ruled that, after April 4, 1971, the Interim Board of Trustees of the Westheimer Independent School District or their successors could pursue their statutory course for the creation and implementation of the district if circumstances changed to the degree that his reasoning for the injunction would no longer be valid. He determined that the interim board must give sixty days notice in writing to all of the parties in the suit.[81] On appeal, the Fifth Circuit determined that the original injunctive decree prohibited the formation of the WISD until it could demonstrate that its formation would not impede the desegregation process in the HISD.[82]

On December 8, 1977, District Judge Finis E. Cowan permanently enjoined the proposed WISD from proceeding further toward the creation and implementation of a splinter school district.[83] The factual findings for this decision were delineated eleven days later.[84] Judge Cowan explained that "both the *contents* and the *method* of preparing the WISD plan demonstrate a lack of responsibility and professional competence."[85]

Circuit Judge Charles Clark affirmed two aspects of this decision. The appeals court held that the division of a district operating under a desegregation order was permissable only if it did not impede the dismantling of a dual school system in the original district. Secondly, the court maintained that the creation of a new district would have a deleterious effect on desegregation of the old district, where its excision would remove 10.5 percent of the total white enrollment of the original district, and would result in the loss of the total tax base. The appellate court vacated the part of the district court's order that permanently prohibited the proponents of the WISD from taking action toward implementing the new district; it ruled that the lower court had abused its discretion.[86]

In litigation relating back to the original Amended Decree of September 18, 1970, District Judge James Noel entered an Order Amending Decree on July 11, 1975.[87] The decree allowed the HISD to unpair the schools paired by the Fifth Circuit in 1970[88] and allowed it to implement a new magnet school plan. The plan included these elements, among others:

1. Phase I would be effective at the beginning of the 1975–76 school year.

2. Phase II would be effective at the beginning of the 1976–77 school year.

3. The elementary schools ordered paired by the Fifth Circuit could be unpaired at the beginning of the 1975–76 school year, with the boundaries of the schools to be restored to the original equidistant zone lines ordered by the district court on June 1, 1970.

4. Racial composition goals would be that no nonmagnet school would be more than 90 percent white or 90 percent black and Hispanic.[89]

Thirty-four magnet programs on thirty-one campuses were implemented in the fall of 1975 (Phase I), and eleven more commenced in the fall of 1976 (Phase II) (Campbell & Brandsetter, 1977: 129). In addition to magnet schools, desegregation techniques included majority to minority transfers and redrawing attendance zones (Rossell & Clarke, 1987: 26).

On June 10, 1980, during the twenty-fourth year of this litigation, District Court Judge Robert O'Conor, Jr., denied the motion of the United States to add new defendants and for leave to file an amended complaint in intervention.[90] The Justice Department had attempted to add twenty-two surrounding school districts, the state of Texas, the Texas Education Agency, the city of Houston, and the Harris County Department of Education as defendants in order to gain approval of an interdistrict desegregation order. O'Conor opined:

The assumption of hard-line adversary positions, which would be taken by the proposed new litigants, would only serve to negate new progress this Court has engineered to date insofar as the voluntary interdistrict plan is concerned and to postpone even further a decision in a case which has cried out for resolution for the past twenty-four years.[91]

Instead, the district court approved of a voluntary interdistrict plan to be implemented in the fall of 1980.[92] The board implemented a plan on schedule, entitled Voluntary Interdistrict Education Plan (VIEP). The plan was formulated by the Texas Education Agency. It authorized tuition waivers and free transportation for students who wished to participate.[93]

On June 17, 1981, O'Conor declared the HISD to be a unitary school district.[94] In his decision he found that the district had done everything practical in achieving this status. The district court officially put the case on the inactive docket for three years. At the end of this period, if no segregative actions had been taken by the district to alter the district's status, the case would be dismissed. This decision was affirmed on appeal by the Fifth Circuit.[95]

The parties involved in the litigation arrived at a settlement agreement on September 10, 1984.[96] Occurring twenty-eight years after the initial suit, the agreement was for five years and can be extended by agreement of the parties. The district court approved of the settlement on November 27, 1984.[97]

JEFFERSON COUNTY/LOUISVILLE, KENTUCKY (JEFFERSON COUNTY PUBLIC SCHOOLS)

Jefferson County Population

1940	385,392
1950	484,615
1960	610,947
1970	695,055
1980	685,004

Louisville Population

1940	319,077
1950	369,129
1960	390,639
1970	361,706
1980	298,451

In compliance with *Brown I*, the Louisville Board of Education banned de jure segregation in 1956. The district received national attention for the peaceful manner in which it implemented the Supreme Court's ruling.[98] Yet by 1971, the Kentucky Commission on Human Rights (1972) reported that racial isolation in Louisville reached a ten-year high during the 1971–72 school year. On June 21, 1971, the U.S. Department of Health, Education, and Welfare ordered the Jefferson County Board of Education to remove the "racial identity" of its virtually all-black Newburg Elementary School. Two months later, the Kentucky Civil Liberties Union (KCLU) and the Legal Aid Society filed suit in the U.S. District Court, requesting desegregation of the Jefferson County school system. On June 22, 1972, the KCLU and the NAACP filed suit requesting desegregation of the Louisville Independent School District (Perley, 1975: 11). At this time, both Jefferson County and the city of Louisville operated separate and distinct school systems. In fact, of the twenty school districts in this study, this is the only case where desegregation efforts involved the merging of two districts.

Chief Judge James F. Gordon of the U.S. District Court for the Western District of Kentucky dismissed both actions, and they were consolidated for appeal.[99] On December 28, 1973, the U.S. Court of Appeals for the Sixth Circuit reversed this decision. Judge William F. Miller ordered both districts to desegregate, finding that neither had achieved a unitary system. Implementation of any desegregation plans was ordered for the 1974–75 school year.[100] The U.S. Supreme Court granted the petition for certiorari and vacated the earlier judgments and remanded the cases for further consideration. On December 11, 1974, the Sixth Circuit reinstated its earlier judgment. Any implemented desegregation proceedings could not occur before the beginning of the 1975–76 school year.[101]

On July 3, 1975, the district court formulated a desegregation plan (thereby rejecting other proposals) that merged the two districts (Louisville Independent School District and Jefferson County Public Schools) into one.[102] Two weeks later, the court of appeals issued a writ of mandamus ordering District Court Judge Gordon to go forward with full-scale implementation of the desegregation plan to take effect at the beginning of the 1975–76 year (approximately two months later). Perley (1975: 14) comments on Gordon's involvement in these cases:

> Perhaps the most crucial elements in the relatively successful implementation of the plan were the strength, courage and leadership exerted by Judge Gordon. Judge Gordon's behavior is all the more remarkable because he had ruled against the original complaint that the two school systems were not desegregated. But having been reversed by the Sixth Circuit Court of Appeals, Judge Gordon showed a determination that a viable desegregation plan be drawn up and implemented. He indicated from the start that he would tolerate no nonsense and that he would call upon all the force necessary to see to it that the plan was implemented. It was Judge Gordon who forced both the mayor and the county judge to take strong action. Until a few days before school was to open, neither of these top elected local officials had shown any inclination to exert leadership or to encourage those forces that were working to achieve peaceful desegregation. Both had indicated that they were against busing but that they would uphold the law. They did this when the time came, but largely because of the strong leadership and prodding by Judge Gordon.

The racial composition goals of the plan provided for no more than 12 to 40 percent minority students in the elementary schools, and no more than 12.5 percent to 35 percent minority students in the secondary schools (Rossell & Clarke, 1987: 24). Techniques included pairing and clustering, the closing of selected schools, and magnet schools (Rossell & Clarke, 1987: 27).

Gordon's plan was upheld on appeal.[103] It was modified two years later when the court of appeals ordered the district court to include first graders in the busing plan.[104] By April 4, 1984, the Jefferson County Board of Education approved its "second generation" desegregation plan (Jefferson County Public Schools, April 4, 1984). This established new racial composition goals—minority enrollment in each school would be between 10 percent above and 10 percent below the countywide average (Jefferson County Public Schools, April 4, 1984). Implementation of this plan was in 1984–85 for high schools and 1985–86 for elementary and middle schools (Jefferson County Public Schools, September 29, 1989).

MILWAUKEE, WISCONSIN (MILWAUKEE PUBLIC SCHOOLS)

City Population

1940	587,472
1950	637,392
1960	741,324
1970	717,099
1980	636,212

Golightly (1963: 27) reports that segregation in Milwaukee during the early 1960s was de facto in nature:

The racial imbalance in Milwaukee's central city schools provides a rare opportunity to observe an "ideal case" of de facto segregation based chiefly on housing patterns. Not only is the predominantly Negro school of recent origin but the metamorphosis of white schools into Negro schools can still be readily observed as the Negro population and neighborhood expand.

In later years, the federal courts would offer another interpretation of segregated schools in Milwaukee.

On January 19, 1976, Chief Judge John W. Reynolds of the U.S. District Court for the Eastern District of Wisconsin issued an injunction against the Milwaukee public schools, holding that segregation was intentionally caused and maintained by the Board of School Directors.[105] The initial suit was brought on September 10, 1973.[106] Reynolds allowed this case to be brought as a class action on behalf of two classes. The first consisted of all black students enrolled in the system at that time as well as those who would enroll in the future. The second group included all nonblack students enrolled in the system at that time as well as those who would enroll in the future. Reynolds declared:

> The Court concludes that the defendants have knowingly carried out a systematic program of segregation affecting all of the city's students, teachers, and school facilities, and have intentionally brought about and maintained a dual school system. The Court therefore holds that the entire Milwaukee public school system is unconstitutionally segregated.[107]

Reynolds also announced that the district court would appoint a special master to assist it in formulating a desegregation plan.[108]

The district court established racial composition goals for the school district on June 11, 1976:[109]

> The number of schools having a student population between 25% to 45% black shall be deemed indicative of the extent of the desegregation of the school system. The plan which the defendants submit should cause at least one-third of the schools to have student populations falling within the foregoing racial range by September 30, 1976, at least an additional one-third of the schools to have student populations within the racial range by September 30, 1977, and the remaining schools to have student populations within that racial range by September 30, 1978.[110]

Indeed, implementation of the Milwaukee plan did occur in three phases: 1976-77 (Phase I); 1977-78 (Phase II); and 1978-79 (Phase III).[111] Techniques included the creation of magnet schools, majority to minority transfers, school closings, and rezoning (Rossell & Clarke, 1987: 26).

The initial order by Chief Judge Reynolds was upheld on appeal by Circuit Judge Tone of the Seventh Circuit Court of Appeals.[112] On remand, the district court found that the district discriminated against minorities with segregative intent and, in so doing, violated the Fourteenth Amendment Equal Protection Clause and the Civil Rights Act of 1871.[113] On May 4, 1979, new racial composition goals were promulgated by the district court:

A "desegregated" school for purposes of student desegregation is defined as:

1. Each elementary or junior high school which has a student population composed of not less than 25% and not more than 60% black students and

2. Each senior high school which has a student population composed of not less than 20% and not more than 60% black students.[114]

A few years later an interesting twist occurred in the litigation battle.

In 1984, the Milwaukee school board brought suit against twenty-four suburban Milwaukee school districts, the governor of Wisconsin (Tommy G. Thompson), and the state superintendent of public instruction (Herbert J. Grover). The case sought an interdistrict school desegregation remedy so that the Milwaukee school system could correct the "unlawful dual structure of education in the Milwaukee metropolitan area."[115] The NAACP later entered the suit as intervening plaintiffs. On August 10, 1987, a settlement was reached between the parties involved (Milwaukee Public Schools, September 16, 1987).

Before discussing this settlement, it is imperative to turn to the state's role in the Milwaukee plan. In declaring its support for voluntary desegregation efforts, the Wisconsin state legislature passed Chapter 220, which was incorporated into the Wisconsin statutes as Chapter 220, Laws of 1975:

> The state of Wisconsin hereby declares that it is the announced policy of the state to facilitate the transfer of students between schools and between school districts to promote cultural and racial integration in education where students and their parents desire such transfer and where schools and school districts determine that such transfers serve educational interests. The state further declares that it is a proper state expense to encourage such transfers through provision of special aids (Conta, 1978: 288–89).

This law provides for both interdistrict and intradistrict transfers of minorities from districts or schools where minority group students constitute 30 percent or more to districts or schools where the minority population is less than 30 percent of total enrollment. It also provides transfers for nonminorities from districts or schools where minority enrollment is less than 30 percent to districts or schools where the minority population is greater than 30 percent of total enrollment. In Milwaukee, Chapter 220 provides state aid for transfers between the city and suburban school districts and from school to school within the Milwaukee public school system (Kritek, 1977: 83).

In the court settlement, the Milwaukee school board maintained that the twenty-four suburbs, the governor, and the state superintendent had failed to help Milwaukee desegregate its schools. The settlement called for increased opportunities for students in Milwaukee to transfer to the outlying suburban districts (Wisconsin Department of Public Instruction, 1988).

Specifically, the Brown Deer, Fox Point, Bayside, Glendale-River Hills, Maple Dale-Indian Hill, and Nicolet school districts agreed to accept Chapter 220 transfers equalling up to 23 percent of their student enrollment, minus the number of minorities who reside in the district and the number of nonminority students who transfer to the Milwaukee school district. Cudahy, Greendale, Greenfield, South Milwaukee, and Whitefish Bay agreed to a 20 percent figure. The Menomonee Falls school district agreed to 13 percent. The other districts (except Muskego-Norway, which was dismissed from the suit) agreed to provide a specific number of seats for Chapter 220 transfers. These suburbs agreed to make a good-faith effort to increase the number of slots available between the 1987–88 and 1992–93 school years. In 1986–87, the year before the settlement, approximately 3,100 minority students from Milwaukee attended suburban schools under Chapter 220. In 1987–88, the first year under the settlement, 3,758 students from Milwaukee went to the suburbs for school, while 905 students from the suburbs went to classes in Milwaukee (Wisconsin Department of Public Instruction, 1988). Thus, although 1987–88 is the first year of implementation of the settlement, Chapter 220 funds were first utilized in Phase I of implementation of the major plan dating back to 1976–77.

MONTCLAIR, NEW JERSEY (MONTCLAIR PUBLIC SCHOOLS)

City Population

1940	39,807
1950	43,927
1960	43,129
1970	44,043
1980	38,321

Movement toward desegregation in the Montclair public schools began in 1960. Black parents were irate because they believed that the junior high school that served their community was clearly inferior in facilities and programs to middle schools in white areas. After five years, this particular junior high school was ultimately closed. Yet districtwide desegregation efforts were thwarted as school bond issues and referenda were defeated in 1962, 1963, 1966, and 1967 (Parelius, 1983: 8–9).

By the fall of 1971, the district had implemented desegregation efforts targeted at grades five through twelve. Techniques included grade reorganization and school pairings between 1971 and 1975 (Rossell & Clarke, 1987: 29). As is true with many school districts undergoing similar change, the greatest controversy remained with desegregating the early elementary schools affecting small children. In 1972, a new superintendent presented a new "Plan of Action." This plan included reorganizing the kindergarten through fourth grade schools with each school missing one grade. For the one year that their neighborhood school did not offer, children would be bused to another school. The school board backed this plan but the city council was adamantly opposed to it. Several other major community groups were against it as well (Parelius, 1983: 9–12).

In 1974, a new acting superintendent was appointed who subsequently presented the school board and the public with several alternative plans for desegregating the rest of the district. His plans were called the "rainbow effort," as each was distinguished by a different color. Several different groups ironed out a politically acceptable plan called the "Revised, Modified Green Plan." This entailed school closings, redistricting, and transportation of elementary age children outside of their neighborhood schools. On July 1, 1976, the school board voted to adopt the plan, and a citizens' advisory task force was created to study the plan and recommend any modifications if necessary (Parelius, 1983: 13–16).

This "Revised, Modified Green Plan" only involved the elementary and middle schools, which were reorganized to achieve greater racial balance. The attendance boundaries of all these schools were eliminated (Rossell & Clarke, 1987: 29). The district also employed a magnet program to attract minority students on one side of town to a predominantly white section and a Gifted and Talented Program to achieve the opposite. The open enrollment (or freedom of choice) feature of the earlier limited desegregation effort in 1967 was retained, allowing parents to send their children to any elementary school in the system as long as such movement did not create a racial imbalance in the district (Parelius, 1983: 16-17). Implementation began in the fall of 1977, and the racial composition goals required between 25 and 57 percent minority students in each school (Rossell & Clarke, 1987: 23).

MONTGOMERY COUNTY, MARYLAND (MONTGOMERY COUNTY PUBLIC SCHOOLS)

County Population

1940	83,912
1950	164,401
1960	340,928
1970	522,809
1980	579,053

Larson (1980) reports that, by 1976, it was apparent that increased desegregation efforts were warranted in the Montgomery County Public Schools (MCPS). He cites the following evidence:

In the eight years from 1960 and 1968, the percentage of the MCPS enrollment which was minority group pupils increased from 4 to 6.5. However, in the eight-year period from 1968 to 1976, the minority enrollment had climbed to 16.4 percent. This percentage of minority pupils was relatively low compared to many large city school systems, where minority enrollments between 50 and 90 percent were becoming increasingly common. Nevertheless, the change in MCPS had come about rather quickly and, more importantly, had not occurred evenly across all schools (p. 1).

Thus, Larson focuses on the changing demographics and population shifts in the district.

The stress on changing demographics is further reiterated in a policy statement made by the district on October 10, 1983:

> Housing patterns in Montgomery County and elsewhere develop as the result of a highly complex combination of economic and market forces, government policies, and individual choices. None of these is under the control of the Board of Education or the public schools. Nevertheless, the Board and the staff have the responsibility to take feasible actions to stem any trend toward racial or ethnic isolation in any school, and they have consistently attempted to do so (Montgomery County Public Schools, 1983).

The school board implemented its desegregation plan beginning in the 1976–77 school year. At that time, racial composition goals were to have no more than 50 percent minority students in any school (Rossell & Clarke, 1987: 24).

The techniques utilized for desegregation included magnet schools, pairing and clustering, and the redrawing of attendance zones (Montgomery County Public Schools, 1983). The magnet schools follow a cluster model, where all the schools are in a feeder pattern in which the elementary and junior high schools feed into a high school (Montgomery County Public Schools, 1988).

PORTLAND, OREGON (PORTLAND PUBLIC SCHOOLS)

City Population

1940	305,394
1950	373,628
1960	372,676
1970	382,619
1980	366,383

The impetus for desegregation in the Portland public schools came largely through the efforts of the local NAACP (United States Commission on Civil Rights, 1977b: 4). On April 20, 1962, it publicly charged that racial segregation existed in the school system and that this created a sense of inferiority among black students that was detrimental to future aspirations and achievements. No specific recommendations were provided by the group at this time (Geddes, 1982: 97–98). In 1963, the Portland Board of Education established an independent citizens' committee on education and race. The group was to study problems of racial isolation and recommend solutions. The committee did so and, in 1964–65, the Portland school board, acting upon these recommendations, implemented a voluntary transfer program called the Administrative Transfer Program, which involved transporting minority students to predominantly white schools (United States Commission on Civil Rights, 1977b: 5).

By 1969, the school district hired a new superintendent, Robert W. Blanchard, to replace Melvin W. Barnes, who resigned (Geddes, 1982: 105). After he assumed his duties, the school board asked him to address a series of issues, one of which was related to racial isolation in the schools (Geddes, 1982: 105–08). On March 23, 1970, the board unanimously adopted Blanchard's *Portland Schools for the Seventies* program. The board formally adopted the following policy:

> That in accordance with policy established in December, 1964, in the adoption of the Report of the Board's Committee on Race and Education, improvement in curriculum, organization, administration and physical plant, and designation of attendance areas, should be carried out in a manner which will achieve the integration of students of all races and reduce concentrations of racial minorities (Portland Public Schools, n.d.: 22).

The plan relied on continuation of the majority to minority transfers, creation of magnet schools, grade level reorganization, and consolidation of certain schools (Rossell & Clarke, 1987: 26). No more than 25 percent minority students were to attend each junior and senior high school, while no more than 50 percent were to attend any given elementary school (Rossell & Clarke, 1987: 23).

By the late 1970s, a group called the Community Coalition for School Integration determined that a districtwide examination of the desegregation plan was in order. This group was formed by the school board, the NAACP, the Urban League, and the Metropolitan Human Relations Commission (Geddes, 1982: 112). The group defined its purpose as that of

> identifying common concerns in the Portland community regarding school desegregation, and developing the kind of policy recommendations that would enhance equal educational opportunities and thereby maximize the potential of every student to achieve (Geddes, 1982: 113).

The coalition produced a report entitled *Equity for the Eighties: A Report to the Board of Education.* Its major finding was that the black community had an unequal share of the burden for desegregation and that this was inequitable (Geddes, 1982: 113). The board responded by approving the "Comprehensive Desegregation Plan" on April 14, 1980 (Portland Public Schools, 1980, 1981). This plan was basically a reaffirmation of the techniques utilized in the plan implemented during the 1970–71 school year (Portland Public Schools, n.d: 25–26). Implementation of the new plan occurred in 1980–81 (Portland Public Schools, 1981: i).

RACINE, WISCONSIN (RACINE UNIFIED SCHOOL DISTRICT)

City Population

1940	67,195
1950	71,193
1960	89,144

1970   95,162
1980   85,725

In 1966, the Racine Unified School District began what some considered initial desegregation efforts. A high school was opened and two predominantly minority junior high schools were closed, with the students redistributed elsewhere in the district. The president of the local NAACP believed, however, that the schools were closed only "for better utilization of facilities available," and not for purposes of desegregation (United States Commission on Civil Rights, 1977a: 2). It was not until 1972 that the local school board began planning to desegregate the entire district. These efforts were thwarted by citizen protest, which resulted in a deferment of action (United States Commission on Civil Rights, 1977a: 2).

This deferment did not last long. Early in the summer of 1973, the Wisconsin Department of Public Instruction sent its state guidelines for desegregation to Racine. The guidelines required all districts in the state to racially balance their schools within 10 percentage points of the proportion of all ethnic groups in their district. In response, the school board proposed a plan that would meet the state's guidelines. The plan was to be implemented in September of 1975. At this time, a Citizens' Advisory Committee was created (United States Commission on Civil Rights, 1977a: 4–5).

Acting on this committee's recommendations, district administrators presented four plans to the school board in July, 1974. The reorganization plan would group each of nine middle schools with three or four elementary schools. In each group, fifth and sixth graders would attend the middle school. The other schools in each group would contain grades one through four. All schools in the group would have kindergartens composed of the children in the neighborhood.

The redistribution plan focused on the state's guidelines, and proposed that the minority students in grades one through six would be transferred from the seven inner-city schools and reassigned to the twenty-three outer-city schools to reach the prescribed percentage (no school shall exceed the district minority percentage by more than 10 percentage points). This plan would allow for magnet programs and would keep kindergartens operating in neighborhood schools.

The exchange plan proposed utilizing all public school facilities to exchange minority students from the seven inner-city schools with the white students from the twenty-three outer-city schools. The percentage of minority students for outer-city schools would be established by the school board. Any additional number of minorities could be added to a school keeping the enrollments at the previous level. This exchange of students would take place whether the kindergarten students were included or not.

Last, the cluster plan proposed that the district be divided into four clusters or organizational patterns of education: modified self-contained, multiunit, nongraded continuous progress, and academic. Parents within each cluster would choose the type of school they wished for their child. Students would be assigned to the schools of their choice based on the shortest distance from their homes and the minority percentage established by the board (United States Commission on Civil Rights, 1977a: 5–6).

On August 14, 1974, the school board adopted the redistribution plan (United States Commission on Civil Rights, 1977a: 7). Full implementation began in the fall of 1975 (United States Commission on Civil Rights, 1977a: 12). The racial composition goal in operation presently for the district is that all schools will be no more than 15 percent above or 10 percent below the overall district average percentage of minorities at the grade levels encompassed (Racine Unified School District, December 19, 1988).

ST. PAUL, MINNESOTA (ST. PAUL PUBLIC SCHOOLS)

City Population

1940   287,736

1950	311,349
1960	313,411
1970	309,980
1980	270,230

In 1964, the St. Paul Public Schools Board of Education adopted an equal opportunity policy that was later amended in 1967 to state:

> The Board recognizes the evidence that concentration of racial groupings in schools from whatever causes is one of the factors which inhibits the educational development of the children involved, and that the existence of de facto segregation is inconsistent with the democratic principle of equality of educational opportunity (St. Paul Public Schools, August 1984: 1–2).

In 1964, the Board of Education appointed a Citizens' Committee to study racial imbalance in the schools. This committee determined that growing racial imbalance was due to the influx of minority families into the district. The following year the board established a nine-member Human Relations Committee and adopted an open enrollment policy for the district (St. Paul Public Schools, August, 1984: 2). Seventy-five junior and senior high school students participated in the program in 1965–66, and seventy-eight more students including elementary school children participated in 1966–67 (Weldin, 1977: 116). All participants were black (Weldin, 1977: 122). The continuing open enrollment policy was altered in August, 1972, so that transfers of students would be accepted only if it would improve the racial balance of the sending and receiving school (Weldin, 1977: 127).

In 1969 and 1970, the St. Paul Commission on Human Rights determined that the school system should provide a desegregation plan for the district. A lawsuit was initiated against the district in 1970 to do this. The superintendent of schools successfully had this suit dismissed by promising to make substantial progress on a plan by September, 1971 (Weldin, 1977: 125).

The State Board of Education cited seven segregated elementary schools in St. Paul on April 13, 1971. The state commissioner of education, Howard Casmey, gave the district ninety days to submit a plan (Weldin, 1977: 125). The district complied and submitted a plan to Casmey. Before he would approve the plan he asked that the St. Paul Board of Education meet with the state board to discuss its feasibility. That meeting was held on August 29, 1971. On April 10, 1972, the commissioner rejected St. Paul's plan and gave the district ninety days to submit a new one (Weldin, 1977: 128–129).

On July 2, 1972, the state provisionally approved the creation of elementary and secondary learning centers as an experiment on a year-to-year basis to give the State Department of Education time for evaluation. A new comprehensive plan was ordered on November 15, 1973. The new revised plan was approved by the State Board of Education on May 13, 1974 (Weldin, 1977: 129). This plan relied mostly on pairing and clustering, consolidation of schools, the redrawing of attendance zones, and magnet schools (Rossell & Clarke, 1987: 27). This major plan was phased in between 1974–75 and 1976–77 (Weldin, 1977: 130). The phases of the plan included the development of elementary clusters: Jupiter, Saturn and Neptune, Saturn and Aquarius, Apollo, Gemini, and Neptune and Aquarius. It also included the development of Webster magnet school and plans to reorganize the secondary schools and institute elementary and secondary learning centers (St. Paul Public Schools, August 1984: 3). Racial composition goals were to have no school more than 30 to 40 percent minority (Rossell & Clarke, 1987: 24).

On March 18, 1983, the commissioner of education, John J. Feda, informed the district that eleven schools were out of compliance with Minnesota State Rule 621c:

Segregation occurs in a public school district when the minority composition of the pupils in any school building exceeds the minority racial composition of the student population of the entire district for the grade levels served by that school building by more than 15% (St. Paul Public Schools, May 22, 1984: 1).

Plans to remedy the racial imbalances in these schools were implemented in 1985–86, and relied on the primary techniques that were implemented during the major plan (St. Paul Public Schools, May 22, 1984: 4–27).

SAN BERNARDINO, CALIFORNIA (SAN BERNARDINO CITY UNIFIED SCHOOL DISTRICT)

City Population

1940	43,646
1950	63,058
1960	91,922
1970	104,251
1980	117,490

In 1966, the San Bernardino City Unified School District allowed the voluntary transfer of minority students to other schools on a space-permitting basis. This controlled open enrollment program was targeted at elementary and junior high schools.[116] The district implemented a partial desegregation plan for its junior and senior high schools in 1970 by redrawing attendance boundaries. The majority of the elementary schools remained segregated, however (Trombley, 1977b: 104). In June 1972, the school district was sued by eight black parents who maintained that dual schools were damaging the equal educational opportunities of their children. On September 13, 1973, Superior Court Judge Paul Egly ruled that the district's elementary schools were segregated and ordered the school board to begin meaningful proceedings toward desegregation by September, 1974.[117]

Judge Egly's decision was overruled by the United States Court of Appeals for the Fourth Circuit.[118] Judge Whyte makes the distinction between de jure and de facto segregation:

> There is no finding that the racial imbalance in the San Bernardino City School system was or is the result of intentional action practiced against the minority students for the purpose of imposing upon them racial segregation. That is to say that there is no holding of de jure segregation, since the finding of intent requisite to such a determination was not made. Lacking such a finding there is no constitutionally imposed duty on the school board to take affirmative steps to eliminate racial imbalance unless such racial imbalance is in fact depriving said minority students of an equal educational opportunity.[119]

Thus, the trial court's judgment was reversed and remanded with the instructions to make findings on two issues. The first issue would be to determine whether or not the racial imbalance in the school district was the result of deliberate intent by the school board; the second would be to determine whether or not the racial imbalance deprived the minority children of equal educational opportunities.[120] If either question were answered in the affirmative, the trial court could reinstate its earlier judgment. Negative findings on both questions would direct the trial court to deny the NAACP a peremptory writ of mandate to direct the district to implement a desegregation plan.[121]

The NAACP appealed the Fourth Circuit's decision and, on June 28, 1976, the California Supreme Court reaffirmed Judge Egly's decision,[122] ordering the San Bernardino City Unified School District to desegregate.[123] Judge Tobriner maintained that, although the controlled open enrollment program did enhance desegregation between 1966 and 1972, statistical analysis of the district revealed that the district had failed to alleviate segregation in several junior high and elementary schools located in minority neighborhoods. The court ruled that the trial court had properly refused to credit the district's claim that de facto, rather than de jure, segregation existed in the district. Tobriner adhered:

> The school district conceded that some of the schools in its district were racially or ethnically imbalanced under the foregoing statutory and administrative provisions, but asserted that any such imbalance was purely de facto in nature and that the district had at all times taken "all measures possible within the limits of the financial resources available to the district" to remedy such imbalance. Under these circumstances, the district claimed that it had complied with all its constitutional or statutory obligations.[124]

The court stressed the importance of all school boards taking steps to alleviate segregation, regardless of the causes of such segregation. Although the Supreme Court reaffirmed the earlier ruling, the case was remanded to the trial court, as it had improperly defined segregation as a result of an earlier case[125]:

> The trial court used a number of alternative formulas in defining "segregation," but all of the formulas identified a "segregated school" on the basis of the school's deviation from a "racial balance" norm; after the trial court's order was filed, our court upheld the constitutionality of the portion of Proposition 21 that repealed the "racial balance" provisions upon which the trial court had relied. In light of this appeal, California schools bear no statutory obligation to achieve racially balanced schools.[126]

The court noted that school districts are only required to take all reasonable and feasible steps to eliminate schools in which minority enrollment is so disproportionate as to isolate minority students from other students and thus deprive them of a desegregated educational experience.

On August 30, 1977, Judge Egly approved the school board's voluntary desegregation plan, which relied on magnet and cluster schools. He instructed the district to submit a back-up mandatory plan relying on forced busing by February 28, 1978, if the voluntary plan failed to achieve desegregation after one year.

Upon doing so, the final plan was approved in May, 1978 (Trombley, 1980: 16–17). The major components of the plan were implemented from 1978–79 to the 1980–81 school year (San Bernardino City Unified School District, 1989). Techniques included majority to minority transfers, magnet schools, school closings, and rezoning (Rossell & Clarke, 1987: 26). No numerical goals were set (Rossell & Clarke, 1987: 23).

SAN DIEGO, CALIFORNIA (SAN DIEGO UNIFIED SCHOOL DISTRICT)

City Population

1940	203,341
1950	334,387
1960	573,224
1970	696,769
1980	875,538

In 1965, the Board of Education of the San Diego Unified School District admitted that de facto segregation "may be a deterrent to equal educational opportunity" (Roeser, 1968: 72). It appointed a Citizens' Committee on Equal Educational Opportunities to review the opportunities available to children from racial or ethnic backgrounds, and to develop proposals for appropriate policies and actions to reduce or eliminate any factors that limit the educational opportunities of these children (Roeser, 1968: 72).

The committee submitted a report to the Board of Education on August 10, 1966. It concluded that "a serious condition of racial/ethnic imbalance" existed in the San Diego school system and offered thirty-nine recommendations for remedial action (Roeser, 1968: 72). Most went largely ignored (Roeser, 1968: 73–74).

Court action to desegregate the San Diego school system was first filed on December 4, 1967.[127] This was largely due to the uncertainty of the California law during those particular years.[128] Under the rulings of *Crawford v. Board of Education of the City of Los Angeles*[129] and *NAACP v. San Bernardino City Unified School District*[130], de facto segregation was sufficient to violate the state's Equal Protection Clause. Because the United States Supreme Court only recognizes de jure segregation as a constitutional violation, the Board of Education sought to dismiss the case. Judge Louis Welsh denied this request, holding that the Supremacy Clause of the Constitution (Article VI) does not preclude a state from granting to its citizens greater rights than those offered under the U.S. Constitution.[131]

At the time of this case, the superior court found twenty-three of the district's schools to be segregated, using the *Crawford* definition ("minority student enrollment is so disproportionate as realistically to isolate minority students from other students and thus deprive minority students of an integrated educational experience").[132] Welsh determined that the district had not undertaken realistic steps to alleviate racial isolation in spite of the implementation of magnet schools, voluntary pairing for urban studies during the summer, voluntary ethnic transfers, and mixed racial outings[133] in 1966 (Welch & Light, 1987: 84). Since then, Welsh determined that the average minority youngster in 1977 was less isolated, partly due to changing social demographics and also the programs established by the district. The evidence demonstrated, however, that the district put forth a rather lackluster effort to overcome its systemwide[134] racial problems.

The Board of Education was ordered to submit a detailed desegregation plan to the court by June 13, 1977. Welsh further ordered that a portion of the plan be implemented immediately (for the 1977–78 school year) and that target dates be designated for those portions of the plan that might be implemented at a later date.[135] Perhaps the issue of greatest controversy between the two parties involved disputes about school desegregation techniques. Some were concerned with the advisability of utilizing mandatory techniques and possibly risking increased "white flight" from the city; others feared that voluntary techniques might fail to fully desegregate the district. Welsh quelled this debate:

> There are reasons to doubt the appropriateness of mass mandatory pupil assignments. From the evidence presented by the parties and gathered by the court while visiting district schools, it appears that such a radical desegregation technique would be harmful to many minority youngsters.[136]

He further contended:

> This court suggests that a city-wide mandatory transfer plan is undesirable because of the potential harm to minority youngsters and the grave risk that a "busing" order will result in resegregation. To avoid misunderstanding, however, the court repeats that limited mandatory assignments to pair schools, establish educational parks or to implement other integrated learning experiences are appropriate and probably essential.[137]

Following Welsh's direction, the Board of Education developed a desegregation plan relying entirely on voluntary techniques— majority to minority voluntary transfers and magnet schools. Abiding by the court's implementation guidelines, the district put part of its plan into effect in 1977–78, and the remaining programs of the major plan were phased in through the 1980–81 school year (San Diego City Schools, 1989). The plan was criticized by the ACLU and the San Diego Urban League for not having any mandatory measures (Jones, 1978: 1). Yet by November 4, 1983, the Superior Court of San Diego County with Judge Franklin Orfield presiding was satisfied with the school board's progress toward desegregating its schools, and effectively closed the case.[138] The district has continued to focus its magnet programs on those schools that remain racially isolated (San Diego City Schools, 1989).

SPRINGFIELD, MASSACHUSETTS
(SPRINGFIELD PUBLIC SCHOOLS)

City Population

1940	149,554
1950	162,399
1960	174,463
1970	163,905
1980	152,319

In 1965, the state legislature of the Commonwealth of Massachusetts passed the first Racial Imbalance Act in the nation. In its original form, the law maintained that school boards had to submit annual statistics to the State Board of Education detailing the percentage of nonwhite students in all public schools. If the State Board of Education determined that racial imbalance existed in a public school, it would require the school board to prepare a plan to eliminate such imbalance. School systems that failed to demonstrate reasonable progress and compliance in balancing schools could suffer loss of state funds (Roberts & George, 1986: 1).

The State Board of Education found Springfield to have a number of racially imbalanced schools. In compliance with the Racial Imbalance Act, the school board submitted plans to be implemented in 1966–67, 1967–68, and 1968–69. These proposals primarily involved school construction and consolidation. Implementation of an open enrollment policy coupled with rezoning did occur for the high schools in 1968–69 (Welch & Light, 1987: 87; Roberts & George, 1986: 1–2). Yet the lack of sufficient progress toward desegregation led to the withholding of General Aid to Education funds by the State Board to Education, as well as litigation in the courts (Roberts & George, 1986: 2).

The district was originally ordered to desegregate its elementary and junior high schools on January 11, 1965, by the U.S. District Court for the District of Massachusetts.[139] Chief Judge

Sweeney found no deliberate intent on the part of school authorities to segregate the races. Since the latter part of the eighteenth century, the elementary and junior high schools had been organized on the neighborhood plan. The district lines were drawn with reference to the location and capacity of the schools involved to take into account the safety and convenience of the children. Nevertheless, Sweeney held that segregation existed in the Springfield system. In his words:

> While the experts did not agree on what constitutes racial imbalance in general, or in Springfield in particular, it is unnecessary to define the term. In the light of the ratio of white to non-white in the total population in the City of Springfield, I do find, however, that a non-white attendance of appreciably more than fifty per cent in any one school is tantamount to segregation.[140]

The court further determined that racially imbalanced schools are not conducive to learning and thus deprive minorities equal educational opportunities. Thus, it upheld the premise in *Brown I* that there is a constitutional duty (under the Fourteenth Amendment Equal Protection Clause) to provide equal educational opportunities for all children in the system.

Later that year, on July 12, 1965, the U.S. Court of Appeals for the First Circuit vacated the district court's order.[141] Chief Judge Aldrich determined that, by the time the suit was instituted (January 1964), the school authorities had already recognized what the district court's order later directed. Aldrich utilized the district court's own reasoning:

> To the credit of the City of Springfield and its school authorities, the School Committee recognized, in September 1963, that racial imbalance did exist in some schools, "that integrated education is desirable," and it resolved to "take whatever action is necessary to eliminate to the fullest extent possible, racial concentration in the schools within the framework of effective educational procedures." Accordingly, it voted to take immediate action to prepare, by March 1964, proposals designed to solve the problem. Unfor-

tunately, this lawsuit intervened and the defendants discontinued whatever work they had been doing pending the outcome of this litigation.[142]

Thus, the district court was directed to dismiss the complaint.

The General Aid to Education funds that were withheld from Springfield by the State Board of Education were released when the School Committee of Springfield sued the commissioner of education.[143] Chief Justice Tauro of the Massachusetts Supreme Judicial Court for Hampden County determined that the concern of the court rested with interpretation of the Massachusetts Racial Imbalance Act. He had this to say of the state's actions:

> It is clear in the instant case that the circumstances were not appropriate for the exercise of this power....The sole reason for the board's actions was that, in achieving racial balance, the Springfield school building program might "burden [b]lack parents and children disproportionately." There is no evidence in the record which indicates that the city's program to construct new schools would operate in a discriminatory fashion....While we recognize that compliance with the statute does not necessarily satisfy the constitutional guaranty of equal protection, it is fundamental in our system of government that courts, and not administrative agencies, must resolve conflicts which may arise between statutory and constitutional provisions.[144]

In addition to directing the State Board of Education to deliver the education monies to Springfield, the court also ruled that Springfield must establish a short-range desegregation plan to be implemented in the fall of 1973 (Roberts & George, 1986: 2).

On May 1, 1974, the Massachusetts Supreme Judicial Court affirmed an order of the State Board of Education that directed the Springfield School Committee to immediately implement a six-district desegregation plan to achieve racial balance by the 1974–75 school year.[145] This plan divided the city into six districts. Five of these districts contained one of the predominantly black, imbalanced inner-city schools; schools in the sixth district were primarily Hispanic and were not included in the plan. Grade structures were also revised through pairing and clustering. Kindergarten children, as is most often the case, were exempt from the plan and attended their neighborhood school (Roberts & George, 1986: 4). The plan was carried out as directed in September, 1974. The racial composition goals were to have no school with more than 50 percent minority students (Rossell & Clarke, 1987: 24). In the fall of 1976, magnet schools were added to the plan as well (Roberts & George, 1986: 4). Three magnets were initially created, all in District VI, the district that was not included in the six district plan (Roberts & George, 1986: 8). District VI students would still be able to attend their neighborhood school, and magnet students would fill the remaining available spaces. In 1977–78, five magnet schools enrolled a total of 316 elementary school children. By 1986–87, this figure increased to 1,123 (Roberts & George, 1986: 17). In 1982–83, magnets were first established for junior high school students. Seventy-three students were enrolled during this first year, and the figure increased to 188 by 1986–87. Thus, in the ten year period from 1977–78 to 1986–87, enrollment in magnet schools rose from 316 to 1,311 (Roberts & George, 1986: 17). The magnets are distinctive in that attendance is not voluntary for all students. In fact, the majority of the students attend on an assigned basis (Glenn, 1979: 56).

Thus, the district has been operating on the six-district plan since the fall of 1976. The Springfield school board is currently considering doing away with this plan and initiating another as early as 1990–91. As one source put it, the six-district plan "is not working as well as it could be" (Springfield Public Schools, 1989).

STOCKTON, CALIFORNIA (STOCKTON UNIFIED SCHOOL DISTRICT)

City Population

1940   54,714

1950	70,853
1960	86,321
1970	107,644
1980	149,779

Muskal and Treadwell (1981) divide the Stockton Unified School District's desegregation history into three phases. The first phase (1966–70) marked a period where the superintendent believed in voluntary desegregation but left his position because of lack of community support. By 1970, the federally funded California Rural Legal Assistance (CLRA) program and the NAACP decided to take court action against the district by filing suit in April, in *Hernandez v. School Board of Stockton Unified School District* (Muskal & Treadwell, 1981: 307).

The second phase (1970–74) marked a period of four years of pretrial maneuvering between the CLRA and the attorney for the district. Judge John Keane of the Superior Court of San Joaquin County ruled that the district deliberately segregated students by race and ordered it to implement a desegregation plan (Muskal & Treadwell, 1981: 310–11). The school board contemplated an appeal, but after a few months set out to comply with Keane's order. The period from 1975 to 1979 covers Muskal and Treadwell's (1981) third phase. Acting on Keane's suggestion, the district implemented a small effort targeted at the three high schools in the fall of 1975.

On April 20, 1976, the school district submitted its "Return to Writ of Mandate: Desegregation Plan." The plan called for implementation at the beginning of the 1977–78 school year. The district proposed that, for each three years after implementation, all schools would be modified to fall within plus or minus 15 percent of the racial makeup of the district (Stockton Unified School District, 1976). This plan was acceptable to Judge Keane with minor modifications. The segregated schools in the system would be paired, where two-campus schools would be created in which grades one through three would be taught at one school and grades four through six in the other school. Busing would be utilized to transport the children involved. Because parental fears were most sensitive toward elementary age children, neighborhood kindergartens were to be retained, and extensive participation by the community was allowed as the board appointed a Citizens' Committee to explore various desegregation techniques (Muskal & Treadwell, 1981: 313).

On March 25, 1980, the school board passed its "Revised Desegregation Plan of the Stockton Unified School District" (Stockton Unified School District, 1980). Magnet schools were added at the elementary level for the 1980–81 school year to enhance the district's desegregation effort.

TACOMA, WASHINGTON (TACOMA PUBLIC SCHOOLS)

City Population

1940	109,408
1950	143,673
1960	147,979
1970	154,581
1980	158,501

In 1961, the superintendent of the Tacoma school district voiced his concern over the developing pattern of de facto segregation in the public schools. Two years later, the teachers' association and school administrators appointed representatives to an ad hoc committee formed to study this problem. Solutions were recommended, but no actions were taken. The lack of progress toward desegregating the school system prompted a local attorney and member of the NAACP to inform the school board that it was its responsibility to educate the Tacoma students in a desegregated setting. In 1964 the school board's subcommittee on desegregation supported the closing of two central city schools that were predominantly black and the rezoning of the district's attendance areas (United States Commission on Civil Rights, 1979a: 5-6). A year later, the school board responded to the subcommittee's recommendations by adopting its policy of "equal educational opportunity," which was defined as "freedom from educational treatment based on race, color, caste, or sex" (United States Commission on Civil Rights, 1979a: 6). Despite this policy effort, the desegregation of the district was rejected by the school board at this time.

A month after the school board's policy statement on equal educational opportunity, the Tacoma branch of the NAACP charged that the district had ignored the problem of segregation by failing to implement the subcommittee's recommendations. It also requested the national NAACP to investigate the district for possible violation of the Civil Rights Act of 1964. The investigation did not occur, but the NAACP's actions did spark the school board to act on this issue (United States Commission on Civil Rights, 1979a: 6-7).

On July 8, 1966, the school board implemented an optional enrollment program for the McCarver Junior High School service area, which was located in the central city. The plan provided for choice of any junior high in the district for sixth graders in the McCarver area; choice of any high school in the district for ninth graders in the McCarver area; and also encouraged any student in the district to attend McCarver Junior High if such transfers would reduce the level of de facto segregation in the district. The school board believed that "the neighborhood school can be maintained while also giving greater freedom to parents to choose the schools that they wish their children to attend" (United States Commission on Civil Rights, 1979a: 8).

Participation in the optional enrollment was scant. One hundred fifty-nine students were eligible to transfer from McCarver Junior High but only twenty-seven did so. Nineteen of the 113 graduates from this middle school chose to attend high, schools that were not located in the central city area (United States Commission on Civil Rights, 1979a: 8).

The school board created a Citizens' Committee to study the feasibility of an open enrollment policy for the entire district at the same time that this limited student assignment plan was implemented. The committee recommended that a districtwide policy be implemented in the fall of 1967. This suggestion, however, was rejected by the school board on June 22, 1967, because of the greater enrollment of students than predicted and the time needed to implement the plan before the fall opening of the public schools. The board did extend the optional enrollment policy of 1966 to include transfers in and out of three more central city schools (besides McCarver)—Bryant, Central, and Stanley (United States Commission on Civil Rights, 1979a: 8). The result was that twenty-three high school students, eighty-two junior high school students, and eighty-six elementary school children were transferred. Of these, 61 percent were minorities (United States Commission on Civil Rights, 1979a: 9).

In April 1968, the school administration developed a plan for districtwide desegregation in the Tacoma school district. It developed a five-point program:

1. Transfer students in McCarver Junior High School to other schools beginning in the fall of 1968, in order to racially balance every junior high school.

2. Convert the McCarver facility to an "exemplary," magnet-type elementary school open to all district students. McCarver and Central elementary students would be automatically enrolled if they wished.

3. Convert the Central Elementary School to a teacher training facility to improve staff skills and racial sensitivities.

4. Transfer sixth graders at Stanley Elementary School to other schools to alleviate overcrowding.

5. Continue monitoring the district's high schools to alleviate segregation as all had 16 percent or less black enrollment (United States Commission on Civil Rights, 1979a: 9–10).

After phasing in gradual desegregation techniques over a few years, full-scale implementation of the five-point program began in the fall of 1968. McCarver was the first of currently twelve magnet schools operating in the district. At the time of district-wide implementation, racial composition goals in the district were that no school could have more than 40 percent minority students (Rossell & Clarke, 1987: 23).

The district now operates from a state directive from the Washington State Board of Education and the Washington State Human Rights Commission. A 1981 Joint Policy Statement regarding public school desegregation states, "Racial violation is a condition existing when the racial composition of students in any school building fails to reflect the racial composition of students for the entire District." The State Board of Education considers racial violation to exist when the combined minority enrollment in a school or program exceeds the districtwide combined minority average by 20 percent, provided that the single minority enrollment of a school or program does not exceed 50 percent of the school enrollment (Tacoma Public Schools, 1989).

TULSA, OKLAHOMA (TULSA PUBLIC SCHOOLS)

City Population

1940	142,157
1950	182,740
1960	261,685
1970	331,638
1980	360,919

Up until the time of *Brown I*, all schools in Tulsa were segregated by race under Oklahoma state law. In the fall of 1955, school attendance zones were redrawn utilizing the "neighborhood" school concept. The new zones did place some blacks in previously all-white schools, and vice versa. The school board effectively reversed this process by instituting a policy allowing any student to transfer from a school in which his or her race was in the minority to a school where his or her race was in the majority upon request of the parents (United States Commission on Civil Rights, 1977c: 35). The board allowed these "minority to majority" transfers until 1965, when the Department of Health, Education, and Welfare demanded their discontinuation (United States Commission on Civil Rights, 1977c: 37).

After passage of the Civil Rights Act of 1964, the district submitted a desegregation plan to the U.S. Commissioner of Education. Even though the plan did little to eliminate racial isolation in the schools, the commissioner approved it on August 31, 1965 (United States Commission on Civil Rights, 1977c: 37). On July 30, 1968, the U.S. attorney general filed suit against the Tulsa Independent School District. The district was charged with four counts of unconstitutional discrimination:

1. Designing school attendance zones in such a manner as to segregate students on the basis of race.
2. Permitting transfers of students that in some instances had the purpose and effect of segregating students on the basis of race.
3. Assigning faculty and staff members among various schools on a racially segregated basis.
4. Constructing new schools and additions to schools on the basis of policies and practices that in some instances had the purpose and effect of segregating students on the basis of race (United States Commission on Civil Rights, 1977c: 38).

On March 25, 1969, Judge Fred Daugherty of the U.S. District Court for the Northern District of Oklahoma dismissed the Justice Department's complaint (United States Commission on Civil Rights, 1977c: 38). According to Daugherty, the neighborhood attendance policy did not violate the Constitution. The court determined that the segregated schools in the system were not a result of intentional board action.

On appeal to the Circuit Court of Appeals for the Tenth Circuit, the district court's judgment was reversed.[146] Chief Judge Lewis reflected on the earlier decision:

> This decision and its supportive reasoning are inconsistent with current constitutional standards and gravely inapposite to the spirit of the cases in which these standards have been enunciated.[147]

The court ruled that the neighborhood school policy constituted a system of state-imposed and state-preserved segregation. The case was remanded to the district court with directions to come up with a realistic and effective desegregation plan.

Despite the court activity, implementation of minor desegregation efforts occurred simultaneously. In December 1968, some school boundaries were redrawn, which affected roughly 5,100 whites and 1,200 blacks (out of 79,990 total enrollment) (United States Commission on Civil Rights, 1977c: 41). A four-point plan was implemented in the fall of 1969. The plan called for the desegregation of faculties based on one black teacher in each predominantly white elementary school, two in each predominantly white secondary school, and a fifty-fifty ratio in predominantly black schools. The second part eliminated transfers on grounds other than those of improving the education or welfare of the student. Desegregating fifteen schools by changing attendance areas and encouraging majority to minority transfers comprised the third part. Lastly, the predominantly white Lindsey elementary school was paired with the predominantly black Douglas school (United States Commission on Civil Rights, 1977c: 43–44).

In December 1970, the board proposed a plan that would increase black enrollment at Hawthorne Elementary from 95.7 percent to 97.9 percent, and change the boundary for Carver Junior High, which would have the effect of adding one white student to the enrollment of 790 blacks. This would decrease the 100 percent black enrollment to 99.8 percent (United States Commission on Civil Rights, 1977c: 45–46).

The district's efforts still focused on preserving the neighborhood concept. On March 1, 1971, the Tulsa Board of Education adopted an Amended Plan of Desegregation. This was similar to the December 1970 plan, with the addition of encouraging voluntary transfers of students from schools in which they were in the majority to schools in which they were in the minority. The Department of Justice found this plan to be unacceptable and proposed a counterplan in June 1971. This plan, in turn, was unacceptable to the Board of Education (United States Commission on Civil Rights, 1977c: 46–47). The board submitted a new plan on July 21, 1971. This retained the elementary school proposal, but two changes were made at the secondary level. A Metro Learning Center was to be established at Washington High School, based on the magnet concept, and Carver Junior High School would close and its area would be divided into noncontiguous zones in order to bus the black students involved into surrounding white junior high schools. District Court Judge Daugherty signed the order, and it was implemented between the 1971–72 (Phase I for the junior high schools) and 1972–73 (Phase II for the elementary schools) school years (see Tulsa Public Schools, 1986).

The district court approved the desegregation plan, and the Department of Justice appealed the ruling that the segregation occurring in five of the predominantly black elementary schools was de facto segregation and was not caused by discriminatory action. A group of intervening appellants joined the Justice Department and asked the court of appeals to reverse the district court's judgment approving the plan for student assignment on the junior and senior high school levels. They maintained that the student assignment plan on the secondary level placed a disproportionate share of the desegregation burden on the black community.[148] The court of appeals affirmed the district court's ruling:

> There is no universal plan for desegregation that will fit the problems of every school district. Neither is it possible to devise a plan that will please everyone. Desegregation plans must be

formulated on a case-by-case basis, and preferably formulated and agreed to by the parties involved. Their validity should not depend on the whim or preferences of members of the federal judiciary. They must be judged by constitutional standards. If they accomplish the desired goal of creating a unified school system, and do so in nondiscriminatory manner, we are constrained to approve them.[149]

A year later the Tenth Circuit Court of Appeals affirmed the district court's decision denying the Board of Education's application for a stay of integration relating to four of the elementary schools (Johnson, Dunbar, Woods, and Bunche). Circuit Court Judge Brithenstein held that the school district's decision on educational priorities did not take precedence over a court mandate requiring desegregation of de jure segregated elementary schools.[150]

Desegregation of the district's high schools became Phase III of desegregation in Tulsa and began in 1973–74, when a plan called for Washington High to become a magnet school with a student body of 1,200—600 black and 600 white. Recruitment for this effort began the preceding spring. White enrollment by the beginning of the year reached approximately 555 (a little less than desired), but the program commenced anyway, with a total of 1,100 students (half white and half black). Those black students who could not be accommodated at Washington were assigned to East Central, Edison, Hale, Mason Memorial, and Rogers, which aided in desegregating the white high schools (United States Commission on Civil Rights, 1977c: 69–71).

Five schools were still a part of the ongoing litigation battle. On April 24, 1975, District Court Judge Frederick Daugherty agreed to allow the construction of a new and larger Emerson Elementary School. The plan was to close the old Emerson and Johnson schools, combine their student bodies, and recruit two hundred white students from across the city. The new school opened in September, 1976 (United States Commission on Civil Rights, 1977c: 73). On October 16, 1979, Daugherty cleared the way to desegregate the remaining four elementary schools (Burroughs, Frost, Hawthorne, and Whitman) in question (Tulsa Public Schools, 1986: 5). Magnet programs were created and put into place for the 1980–81 school year (Welch & Light, 1987: 89). The litigation ceased on November 9, 1983, when Daugherty closed the case, declaring that the Tulsa school district had achieved a unitary school status.[151]

A NEW ANALYTICAL FOCUS

Previous research has generated mixed results when comparing differing intervention strategies. Perhaps this is partly due to the classification scheme of school desegregation plans and ensuing operationalization that researchers have relied upon. The following will serve as a synopsis of the descriptive analysis and will provide a new framework for assessing the effectiveness of differing types of desegregation orders.

Rethinking the Mandatory/Voluntary
Operational Dichotomy

Previous research has obviously categorized the school desegregation plans analyzed in a dichotomous fashion: mandatory and voluntary. As the preceding review of the literature indicates, no consensus exists concerning the relative effectiveness of intervention strategies. In fact, utilization of the mandatory and voluntary intervention dichotomy is widespread in the literature, yet confusion still persists regarding the differing typologies of school desegregation plans.

Rossell and Clarke (1987) present a simple 2 × 2 table in which desegregation plans are classified into four types. The source of the order is at the top and divided into two cells: board ordered, and court or Health, Education, and Welfare (HEW) ordered. The degree of parental choice (no choice— mandatory reassignment or choice—voluntary reassignment) is on the left:

Types of Desegregation Plans

Source of Order

Parental Choice	Board (Internal)	Court or HEW (External)
No (Mandatory Reassignment)	1	2
Yes (Voluntary Reassignment)	3	4

Source: Rossell & Clarke (1987: 3)

As Rossell and Clarke (1987) assert, most observers of school desegregation categorize court ordered plans as mandatory and board ordered plans as voluntary. Yet some board ordered plans are mandatory, because they require children to participate as long as they remain in the public school district. On the other hand, some court ordered plans are voluntary, because they allow parental choice as to whether their children are to be reassigned to a desegregated school or to remain in their neighborhood school.

Because of an operational ambiguity in identifying types of interventions, more research would assist policy makers and educators in adopting or even modifying an already existing plan in order to achieve the most effective strategy for their district. Rossell and Clarke (1987: 28) fuel this assertion by stating that

> although we have classified the school districts into two exclusive categories for analytical purposes—mandatory and voluntary, it may be more accurate to describe the mandatory-voluntary dimension in terms of a continuum.

A reconceptualization of this dichotomy and the ensuing measurement strategy have not received sufficient attention to provide distinctions that would go beyond the simple dichotomy. Rossell and Clarke's (1987) study builds on Royster, Baltzell, & Simmons' (1979) examination of magnet schools. Yet the two studies differ in the classification of mandatory and voluntary school desegregation plans:

> Because of the fact that the districts with voluntary plans use some mandatory techniques and the mandatory plans do not encompass all schools as well as the fact that the plans have changed somewhat over time, there will always be some disagreement as to exactly how to classify each of these plans. For example, although this study builds on the 1979 Abt Associates study, we disagree with their classification of three school districts (Rossell & Clarke, 1987: 28).

Just as Rossell and Clarke (1987) did in their study, Smylie (1983) classifies school districts into mandatory and voluntary categories by determining whether or not they rely primarily on forced student reassignment or voluntary strategies to reduce segregation. By formulating a continuum, policy makers and educators will perhaps understand better how their district compares with others of similar enrollments and demographics in terms of desegregation techniques.

An Alternative Classification Scheme

Table 3.1 is a breakdown of Rossell and Clarke's (1987) classification scheme of twenty school districts nationwide. All of the districts in the sample have magnet schools as a component of their plan. Rossell and Clarke (1987) explain that a magnet-voluntary plan is one where desegregation occurs through primarily voluntary transfers. Such plans are typically characterized by voluntary white transfers to magnet schools in minority neighborhoods and voluntary minority transfers to previously white schools that are now magnet schools or under an M to M program. Many also include redrawing of contiguous attendance zones. A magnet-mandatory plan, on the other hand, is one where desegregation is primarily accomplished through the mandatory assignment of students to opposite-race schools. Under mandated

Table 3.1
Rossell and Clarke's (1987) Classification Scheme of Twenty Districts

Magnet-Voluntary

1. Buffalo, New York (Buffalo Public Schools)
2. Cincinnati, Ohio (Cincinnati Public Schools)
3. Houston, Texas (Houston Independent School District)
4. Milwaukee, Wisconsin (Milwaukee Public Schools)
5. Montclair, New Jersey (Montclair Public Schools)
6. Portland, Oregon (Portland Public Schools)
7. San Bernardino, California (San Bernardino City Unified School District)
8. San Diego, California (San Diego Unified School District)
9. Tacoma, Washington (Tacoma Public Schools)

Magnet-Mandatory

1. Boston, Massachusetts (Boston Public Schools)
2. Dallas, Texas (Dallas Independent School District)
3. Dayton, Ohio (Dayton Public Schools)
4. Des Moines, Iowa (Des Moines Independent Community School District)
5. Louisville/Jefferson County, Kentucky (Jefferson County Public Schools)
6. Montgomery County, Maryland (Montgomery County Public Schools)
7. Racine, Wisconsin (Racine Unified School District)
8. St. Paul, Minnesota (St. Paul Public Schools)
9. Springfield, Massachusetts (Springfield Public Schools)
10. Stockton, California (Stockton Unified School District)
11. Tulsa, Oklahoma (Tulsa Public Schools)

Source: Rossell & Clarke (1987: 23–24).

assignment, magnet schools are utilized to reduce conflict and increase parental satisfaction with the primary objective (desegregating the school district). Participation in the magnet school portion of the plan is on a voluntary basis (Rossell & Clarke, 1987: 21–22).

Included in Table 3.2 is a description of the desegregation techniques utilized in the twenty districts discussed above. Magnet schools are a component of all the plans. Given the discrepancies in research findings to date, perhaps researchers should focus more on the operationalization of the interventions involved before measuring their impact on the reduction of segregation. With this in mind, the following carries out Rossell and Clarke's (1987: 28) noteworthy suggestion.

Table 3.2
Desegregation Techniques in Twenty School Districts[a]

District and Implementation Year(s)	Techniques Besides Magnet Schools
Boston (1974/75-1977/78)	Redrawing District Boundaries Reassignment by Geocodes Pairing
Buffalo (1976/77-1981/82)	M to M Transfers Redrawing Attendance Zones Grade Level Reorganization (Elimination of all Middle Schools) Pairing of 20 Zone Schools in 1981
Cincinnati (1973/74-1976/77)	M to M Transfers School Closings Rezoning
Dallas I (1971-72)	Redrawing Attendance Zones M to M Transfers Grade Level Reorganization Pairing and Clustering
Dallas II (1976/77-1980/81)	Redrawing Attendance Zones M to M Transfers Grade Level Reorganization Pairing and Clustering
Dayton (1976-77)	Redrawing Attendance Zones Pairing and Clustering Grade Level Reorganization
Des Moines (1977-78)	M to M Transfers Redrawing Attendance Zones Pairing and Clustering School Closings
Houston I (1970-71)	M to M Transfers Redrawing Attendance Zones Pairing
Houston II (1975/76-1976/77)	M to M Transfers Redrawing Attendance Zones
Louisville/ Jefferson County (1975-76)	Pairing and Clustering School Closings
Milwaukee (1976/77-1978/79)	M to M Transfers School Closings Rezoning

Table 3.2 (continued)

District and Implementation Year(s)	Techniques Besides Magnet Schools
Montclair I (1971-72)	Grade Level Reorganization Pairing
Montclair II (1977-78)	School Closings Elimination of all Attendance Zones Open Enrollment
Montgomery County (1976-77)	Redrawing Attendance Zones Pairing and Clustering
Portland I (1970-71)	M to M Transfers Grade Level Reorganization Consolidation of Certain Schools
Portland II (1980-81)	M to M Transfers Grade Level Reorganization Consolidation of Certain Schools
Racine (1975-76)	Redrawing Attendance Zones
St. Paul (1974/75-1976/77)	Redrawing Attendance Zones Pairing and Clustering Consolidation of Certain Schools
San Bernardino (1978/79-1980/81)	M to M Transfers School Closings Rezoning
San Diego (1977/78-1980/81)	M to M Transfers
Springfield (1974/75-1976/77)	Redrawing Attendance Zones Grade Level Reorganization School Closings
Stockton (1975/76-1980/81)	Pairing and Clustering School Closings
Tacoma (1968-69)	School Closings Districtwide Optional Enrollment
Tulsa (1971/72-1973/74)	M to M Transfers Redrawing Attendance Zones Pairing and Clustering (Dismantled Fall 1985)

Sources: Rossell & Clarke (1987: 26-27); compiled by Author.

[a]Dallas, Houston, Montclair, and Portland all implemented two distinctive desegregation plans.

The Choice-Coercion Continuum

To address questions about the feasibility of utilizing freedom of choice or coercive measures in school desegregation implementation, one might question how much choice or how much coercion is required to successfully desegregate urban school districts. What is the effect of a combination thereof? When examining the twenty districts in question, it becomes apparent that a great deal of variation exists, rather than simply a dichotomy (mandatory and voluntary). It is striking that some desegregation plans utilized more coercive tactics than others on the mandatory side, while some allowed for greater levels of choice on the voluntary side.

One end of the continuum in Figure 3.1 is labelled "Absolute Freedom of Choice for Parents." This extreme is limited by such realities as resources, time, and space. For example, in large urban school districts, a two-hour, one-way bus trip for students may be considered too costly and an inefficient utilization of time. The school of choice for a parent may be limited by space considerations—enrollments may be full, which would force the parent to select another school. Other constraints may be imposed on parents by the districts for racial balance concerns, as well. The other extreme is labelled "Absolute Coercion by School District." This would imply the complete absence of choice by parents as to where their children attend school. This extreme assumes, however, that the parent will choose to remain in the public school district. If, indeed, this is the case, parents must send their children to schools assigned by the district. Assignment rules for the four positions on the continuum obviously reflect the techniques utilized to desegregate (refer back to Table 3.2). The four intervention types are delineated as follows.

High Level of Choice

Districts categorized at this point on the continuum have implemented strictly voluntary techniques to desegregate. Among

Figure 3.1
Choice-Coercion Continuum for Twenty Districts[a]

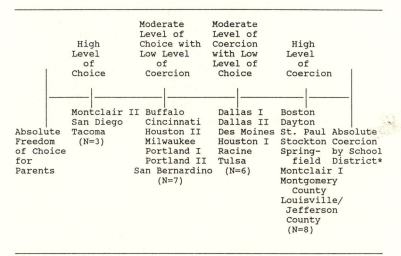

	High Level of Choice	Moderate Level of Choice with Low Level of Coercion	Moderate Level of Coercion with Low Level of Choice	High Level of Coercion	
Absolute Freedom of Choice for Parents	Montclair II San Diego Tacoma (N=3)	Buffalo Cincinnati Houston II Milwaukee Portland I Portland II San Bernardino (N=7)	Dallas I Dallas II Des Moines Houston I Racine Tulsa (N=6)	Boston Dayton St. Paul Stockton Spring- field Montclair I Montgomery County Louisville/ Jefferson County (N=8)	Absolute Coercion by School District*

Note: Parents may choose to relocate and leave the public district altogether, or enroll their children in a private school.

[a]Dallas, Houston, Montclair, and Portland all implemented two distinctive desegregation plans.

these are magnet schools, M to M transfers, optional enrollment, and the elimination of attendance zones. These include Montclair II, San Diego, and Tacoma.

Moderate Level of Choice with Low Level of Coercion

This intervention type is represented by districts that have implemented primarily voluntary techniques to desegregate, but secondarily employ coercive techniques, as well. Those categorized at this point on the continuum have all utilized magnet schools and M to M transfers, but have also implemented coercive measures such as rezoning, the redrawing of attendance zones, and pairing. Among these are Buffalo, Cincinnati, Houston II, Milwaukee, Portland I and II, and San Bernardino.

Moderate Level of Coercion with Low Level of Choice

In contrast to the previous intervention types, this category is dominated by districts that utilize primarily coercive techniques to desegregate, but secondarily employ voluntary techniques, as well. These districts have provided for the redrawing of attendance zones and implementation of pairing and clustering. These are common mandatory techniques that do not allow for parental choice. At the same time, however, voluntary measures including magnet schools and M to M transfers are also included in these plans. Dallas I and II, Des Moines, Houston I, Racine, and Tulsa are represented on this point of the continuum.

High Level of Coercion

Districts categorized at this point on the continuum have implemented strictly coercive techniques to desegregate. These include the redrawing of attendance zones and pairing and clustering. Magnet schools are utilized, but their true purposes are to minimize white resistance to the plan and assumed "white flight," not to allow for parental choice. Among these are Boston, Dayton, Louisville/Jefferson County, Montclair I, Montgomery County, St. Paul, Springfield, and Stockton.

It is important to remember Rossell and Clarke's (1987: 28) words:

> Because of the fact that the districts with voluntary plans use some mandatory techniques and the mandatory plans do not encompass all schools, as well as the fact that the plans have changed somewhat over time, there will always be some disagreement as to exactly how to classify each of these plans.

This is not a process of absolutes. The continuum seemingly affirms Rossell and Clarke's (1987) operational dichotomy, yet adds to the choice versus coercion debate by distinguishing between those plans with extremely high levels of choice or coercion and those that combine various desegregation techniques. By accounting for more variation between and among techniques, it will be easier to determine the most feasible intervention strategy in school desegregation policy.

SUMMARY

Upon examining the mandatory-voluntary dichotomy, it becomes apparent that a great deal of variation exists when classifying types of desegregation plans. The analytical framework presented here attempts to capture this variation more accurately, in order to address the issue of choice versus coercion in school desegregation implementation. At what point on the continuum do desegregation plans facilitate the greatest reduction of segregation? This question can now be addressed.

NOTES

1. 1940, 1950, and 1960 Census: U.S. Department of Commerce, Bureau of the Census, *1960 Census of Population*, Vol. 1, P. A (Washington, D.C.: U.S. Government Printing Office, 1961); 1970 Census: U.S. Department of Commerce, Bureau of the Census, *Characteristics of the Population*, Vol. 1 (Washington, D.C.: U.S. Government Printing Office, 1973); 1980 Census: U.S. Department of Commerce, Bureau of the Census, *Characteristics of the Population*, Vol. 1 (Washington, D.C.: U.S. Government Printing Office, 1983).

2. The reader might be interested in the following accounts: Emmett Buell, Jr., and Richard A. Brisbin, Jr., *School Desegregation and Defended Neighborhoods: The Boston Controversy* (Lexington: D.C. Heath, 1982); Pamela Bullard, Joyce Grant, and Judith Stoia, "Boston, Massachusetts: Ethnic Resistance to a Comprehensive Plan," in Charles V. Willie and Susan L. Greenblatt (Eds.), *Community Politics and Educational Change: Ten School Systems Under Court Order* (New York: Longman, 1981), 31–63; Charles W. Case, "History of the Desegregation Plan in Boston,"

in Daniel U. Levine and Robert J. Havighurst (Eds.), *The Future of Big-City Schools: Desegregation Policies and Magnet Alternatives* (Berkeley: McCutchan, 1977), 153-76; Robert A. Dentler, "Educational Implications of Desegregation in Boston," in Levine and Havighurst (Eds.), *The Future of Big-City Schools,* 177-91; Robert A. Dentler, "The Boston School Desegregation Plan," in Charles V. Willie (Ed.), *School Desegregation Plans That Work* (Westport, Conn.: Greenwood Press, 1984), 59-80; Robert A. Dentler and Marvin B. Scott, *Schools On Trial: An Inside Account of the Boston Desegregation Case* (Cambridge, Mass.: Abt Books, 1981); Jon Hillson, *The Battle of Boston* (New York: Pathfinder, 1977); J. Brian Sheehan, *The Boston School Integration Dispute: Social Change and Legal Maneuvers* (New York: Columbia University Press, 1984); Ralph R. Smith, "Boston: Two Centuries and Twenty-Four Months: A Chronicle of the Struggle to Desegregate the Boston Public Schools," in Howard I. Kalodner and James J. Fishman (Eds.), *Limits Of Justice: The Courts' Role In School Desegregation* (Cambridge, Mass.: Ballinger, 1978), 25-113; and D. Garth Taylor, *Public Opinion and Collective Action: The Boston School Desegregation Conflict* (Chicago: University of Chicago Press, 1986).

3. *School Committee of Boston v. Board of Education,* 363 Mass. 20 (1973).

4. Ibid., at 21-22.

5. Ibid., at 30-31.

6. *School Committee of Boston v. Board of Education,* 364 Mass. 199 (1973).

7. Ibid., at 201.

8. *School Committee of Boston v. Board of Education,* 363 Mass. 125 (1973).

9. *School Committee of Boston v. Board of Education,* 364 Mass. 199 (1973).

10. Ibid., at 207.

11. *Morgan v. Hennigan,* 379 F. Supp. 410 (D. Mass. 1974).

12. Ibid., at 480.

13. Ibid., at 482-84. For a detailed description of Boston during Phase I (1974-75), see Freedom House Institute on Schools and Education, *Boston Desegregation: The First Term, 1974-75 School*

Year (Roxbury: Freedom House Institute on Schools and Education, February 22, 1975), ERIC Document ED 123 280.

14. *Morgan v. Kerrigan*, 509 F.2d 580 (1st Cir. 1974).

15. Ibid., at 598.

16. For a detailed analysis of Boston during Phase II (1975–76), see Massachusetts Research Center, *Education and Enrollments: Boston During Phase II* (Boston: Massachusetts Research Center, 1976).

17. *Morgan v. Kerrigan*, U.S. District Court, D. Mass., May 10, 1975. (Student Desegregation Plan) No. 72–911–G.

18. Ibid., at 7–8.

19. Ibid., at 43–68.

20. *Morgan v. Kerrigan*, 530 F.2d 401 (1st Cir. 1976).

21. *Morgan v. McDonough*, 689 F.2d 265 (1st Cir. 1982), at 269.

22. Ibid.

23. Ibid., at 269–70.

24. Ibid., at 270.

25. Ibid.

26. Ibid.

27. Ibid.

28. Ibid., at 270–71.

29. Ibid.

30. Ibid.

31. Ibid.

32. *Morgan v. Nucci*, U.S. District Court, D. Mass., September 3, 1985. (UFP Orders) No. 72–911–G.

33. *Morgan v. Nucci*, U.S. District Court, D. Mass., September 3, 1985. (Final Orders) No. 72–911–G, at 2–3.

34. Goodwin, Procter, and Hoar, Memorandum to President and Members, Boston School Committee, and Superintendent of Schools, Laval S. Wilson, October 14, 1987, at 1–5.

35. *Arthur v. Nyquist*, 415 F. Supp. 904 (W.D.N.Y. 1976).

36. Ibid., at 911.

37. Ibid., at 911–12.

38. Ibid., at 969.

39. *Arthur v. Nyquist*, 547 F.2d 7 (2d Cir. 1976).

40. *Arthur v. Nyquist*, 429 F. Supp. 206 (W.D.N.Y. 1977).

41. *Arthur v. Nyquist*, 573 F.2d 134 (2nd Cir. 1978).

42. *Board of Education of the City School District of the City of Cincinnati v. Department of Health, Education, and Welfare, Region 5*, 396 F. Supp. 203 (S.D. Oh. 1975).

43. *Board of Education of the City School District of the City of Cincinnati v. Department of Health, Education, and Welfare, Region 5*, 532 F.2d 1070 (6th Cir. 1976).

44. *Bronson v. Board of Education of the City School District of Cincinnati*, 525 F.2d 344 (6th Cir. 1975).

45. Ibid., at 347.

46. *Bronson v. Board of Education of the City School District of the City of Cincinnati*, 604 F. Supp. 68 (S.D. Oh. 1984).

47. For an in-depth timeline of desegregation in Dallas from 1955 to 1976, see Dallas Independent School District, *Desegregation Matrix, 1955 to 1976* (Dallas: Dallas Independent School District, n.d.b). For the period 1976 to 1982, see Dallas Independent School District, *Desegregation Matrix, 1976 and 1982 Orders* (Dallas: Dallas Independent School District, n.d.c).

48. *Tasby v. Estes*, 342 F. Supp. 945 (N.D. Tex. 1971).

49. Ibid., at 950.

50. Ibid., at 953–57.

51. Ibid., at 955–57.

52. *Tasby v. Estes*, 517 F.2d 92 (5th Cir. 1975).

53. Ibid., at 103.

54. Ibid., at 104.

55. *Tasby v. Estes*, 412 F. Supp. 1185 (N.D. Tex. 1975).

56. *Tasby v. Estes*, 572 F.2d 1010 (5th Cir. 1978).

57. *Tasby v. Estes*, 412 F. Supp. 1192 (N.D. Tex. 1975).

58. Ibid., at 1212–1221.

59. *Tasby v. Wright*, 542 F. Supp. 134 (N.D. Tex. 1981).

60. Ibid., at 138–54.

61. *Tasby v. Wright*, 585 F. Supp. 453 (N.D. Tex. 1984).

62. *Tasby v. Black Coalition To Maximize Education*, 771 F.2d 849 (5th Cir. 1985).

63. *Tasby v. Wright*, 630 F. Supp. 597 (N.D. Tex. 1986).

64. *Board of Education of School District of Dayton v. State ex rel. Reese*, 114 Ohio St. 188, 189, 151 N.E. 39 (1926).

65. *Brinkman v. Gilligan*, 503 F.2d 684 (6th Cir. 1974).

66. Ibid.

67. Ibid.

68. *Brinkman v. Gilligan*, 518 F.2d 853 (6th Cir. 1975).

69. *Brinkman v. Gilligan*, 539 F.2d 1084 (6th Cir. 1976).

70. *Dayton Board of Education v. Brinkman* (Dayton I), 433 U.S. 406, 53 L. Ed. 2d 851, 97 S. Ct. 2766 (1977).

71. *Brinkman v. Gilligan*, 446 F. Supp. 1232 (S.D. Oh. 1977).

72. *Brinkman v. Gilligan*, 583 F.2d 243 (6th Cir. 1978).

73. *Dayton Board of Education v. Brinkman* (Dayton II), 443 U.S. 526, 61 L. Ed. 2d 720, 99 S. Ct. 2971 (1979).

74. The Department of Health, Education, and Welfare (HEW) was created on April 11, 1953. It was redesignated as the Department of Health and Human Services (HHS) by the Department of Education Organization Act (93 Stat. 695; 20 U.S.C. 3508), approved on October 17, 1979.

75. *Ross v. Eckels*, 317 F. Supp. 512 (S.D. Tex. 1970).

76. *Ross v. Eckels*, 434 F.2d 1140 (5th Cir. 1970).

77. *Ross v. Eckels*, U.S. District Court, S.D. Tex., Houston Div., September 18, 1970. (Amended Decree) No. 10444.

78. *Ross v. Eckels*, U.S. District Court, S.D. Tex., Houston Div., August 6, 1971. (Memorandum) No. 10444.

79. *Ross v. Houston Independent School District*, U.S. District Court, S.D. Tex., Houston Div., April 4, 1973. (Memorandum And Order) No. 10444.

80. Ibid., at 13.

81. *Ross v. Houston Independent School District*, U.S. District Court, S.D. Tex., Houston Div., April 27, 1973. (Injunction Decree) No. 10444, at 2.

82. *Ross v. Houston Independent School District*, 559 F.2d 937 (5th Cir. 1977).

83. *Ross v. Houston Independent School District*, U.S. District Court, S.D. Tex., Houston Div., December 8, 1977. (Injunction Decree) No. 10444.

84. *Ross v. Houston Independent School District*, 457 F. Supp. 18 (S.D. Tex. 1977).

85. Ibid., at 19.

86. *Ross v. Houston Independent School District*, 583 F.2d 712 (5th Cir. 1978).

87. *Ross v. Houston Independent School District*, U.S. District Court, S.D. Tex., Houston Div., July 11, 1975. (Order Amending Decree) No. 10444.

88. See Note 76.

89. *Ross v. Houston Independent School District*, U.S. District Court, S.D. Tex., Houston Div., July 11, 1975. (Order Amending Decree) No. 10444, at 2–3.

90. *Ross v. Houston Independent School District*, U.S. District Court, S.D. Tex., Houston Div., June 10, 1980. (Memorandum And Order) No. 10444.

91. Ibid., at 12.

92. Ibid., at 12.

93. *Ross v. Houston Independent School District*, U.S. District Court, S.D. Tex., Houston Div., June 17, 1981. (Memorandum And Order) No. 10444, at 32–33.

94. Ibid.

95. *Ross v. Houston Independent School District*, 699 F.2d 218 (5th Cir. 1983).

96. *Ross v. Houston Independent School District*, U.S. District Court, S.D. Tex., Houston Div., September 10, 1984. (Settlement Agreement) No. 10444.

97. *Ross v. Houston Independent School District*, U.S. District Court, S.D. Tex., Houston Div., November 27, 1984. (Order Approving Settlement Agreement) No. 10444.

98. See Kentucky Commission on Human Rights, *Louisville School System Retreats to Segregation: A Report on Public Schools in Louisville, Kentucky, 1956–1971* (Louisville: Kentucky Commission on Human Rights, 1972); United States Commission on Civil Rights, *School Desegregation In Louisville And Jefferson County, Kentucky* (Washington, D.C.: U.S. Government Printing Office, 1976); and Martin M. Perley, "The Louisville Story," *Integrated Education* 13, no. 6 (1975): 11–14.

99. *Newburg Area Council, Inc. v. Board of Education of Jefferson County, Kentucky*, 489 F.2d 925 (6th Cir. 1973).

100. Ibid.

101. *Newburg Area Council, Inc. v. Board of Education of Jefferson County, Kentucky*, 510 F.2d 1358 (6th Cir. 1974).

102. *Newburg Area Council, Inc. v. Board of Education of Jefferson County, Kentucky*, U.S. District Court, W.D. Ky., Louisville, July 3, 1975. Nos. 7045 and 7291 (Exhibit A).

103. *Cunningham v. Grayson*, 541 F.2d 538 (6th Cir. 1976).

104. *Haycraft v. Board of Education of Jefferson County, Kentucky*, 585 F.2d 803 (6th Cir. 1978).
105. *Amos v. Board of School Directors of the City of Milwaukee*, 408 F. Supp. 765 (E.D. Wi. 1976).
106. Ibid., at 777.
107. Ibid., at 821.
108. Ibid., at 822–824.
109. *Armstrong v. O'Connell*, 416 F. Supp. 1344 (E.D. Wi. 1976).
110. Ibid., at 1346.
111. See David A. Bennett. "Community Involvement in Desegregation: Milwaukee's Voluntary Plan," Paper presented at the 1978 annual meeting of the American Educational Research Association, March 27, 1978, Toronto, Ontario, Canada. ERIC Document ED 154 089; and Michael Barndt, Rick Janka, and Harold Rose, "Milwaukee, Wisconsin: Mobilization for School and Community Cooperation," in Charles V. Willie and Susan L. Greenblatt (Eds.), *Community Politics and Educational Change: Ten School Systems Under Court Order* (New York: Longman, 1981), 237–59.
112. *Armstrong v. Brennan*, 539 F.2d 625 (7th Cir. 1976).
113. *Armstrong v. O'Connell*, 451 F. Supp. 817 (E.D. Wi. 1978).
114. *Armstrong v. Board of School Directors of the City of Milwaukee*, 471 F. Supp. 800 (E.D. Wi. 1979), at 807.
115. See *Board of School Directors of the City of Milwaukee v. State of Wisconsin*, 102 F.R.D. 596 (E.D. Wi. 1984), at 598.
116. *NAACP v. San Bernardino City Unified School District*, 46 Cal., App. 3d 49, 119 Cal. Rptr. 784, 551 P.2d 48 (1975).
117. *NAACP v. San Bernardino City Unified School District*, Superior Court of California, County of San Bernardino, September 13, 1973. (Judgment For Petitioners) No. 155286.
118. *NAACP v. San Bernardino City Unified School District*, 46 Cal. App. 3d 49, 119 Cal. Rptr. 784, 551 P. 2d 48 (1975).
119. Ibid.
120. Ibid.
121. Ibid.
122. *NAACP v. San Bernardino City Unified School District*, Superior Court of California, County of San Bernardino, September 13, 1973. (Judgment For Petitioners) No. 155286.

123. *NAACP v. San Bernardino City Unified School District*, 17 C.3d 311, 130 Cal. Rptr. 744, 551 P.2d 48 (1976).

124. Ibid.

125. *Crawford v. Board of Education of the City of Los Angeles*, 17 C.3d 280, 130 Cal. Rptr. 724, 551 P.2d 28 (1976).

126. *NAACP v. San Bernardino City Unified School District*, 17 C.3d 311, 130 Cal. Rptr. 744, 551 P.2d 48 (1976).

127. *Carlin v. Board of Education*, Superior Court of California, County of San Diego, March 9, 1977. (Memorandum Decision And Order) No. 303800, at 1.

128. Ibid.

129. 17 C.3d 280, 130 Cal. Rptr. 724, 551 P.2d 28 (1976).

130. 17 C.3d 311, 130 Cal. Rptr. 744, 551 P.2d 48 (1976).

131. *Carlin v. Board of Education*, Superior Court of California, County of San Diego, March 9, 1977. (Memorandum Decision And Order) No. 303800, at 4.

132. See *Crawford v. Board of Education of the City of Los Angeles*, 17 C.3d 280, 130 Cal. Rptr. 724, 551 P.2d 28 (1976).

133. *Carlin v. Board of Education*, Superior Court of California, County of San Diego, March 9, 1977. (Memorandum Decision And Order) No. 303800, at 6.

134. Ibid., at 17.

135. Ibid.

136. Ibid., at 22.

137. Ibid., at 24.

138. *Carlin v. Board of Education*, Superior Court of California, County of San Diego, November 4, 1983. (Order Re Integration Plan 1983–84) No. 303800.

139. *Barksdale v. Springfield School Committee*, 237 F. Supp. 543 (D. Mass. 1965).

140. Ibid., at 544.

141. *Springfield School Committee v. Barksdale*, 348 F.2d 261 (1st Cir. 1965).

142. Ibid., at 264–65.

143. *School Committee of Springfield v. Board of Education*, 362 Mass. 417 (1972).

144. Ibid., at 431.

145. *School Committee of Springfield v. Board of Education*, 365 Mass. 215 (1974).

146. *U.S. v. Board of Education, Independent School District No. 1, Tulsa County, Oklahoma*, 429 F.2d 1253 (10th Cir. 1970).

147. Ibid., at 1255.

148. See *U.S. v. Board of Education, Independent School District No. 1, Tulsa County, Oklahoma*, 459 F.2d 720 (10th Cir. 1972) at 722; and U.S. Commission on Civil Rights, *School Desegregation in Tulsa, Oklahoma* (Washington, D.C.: U.S. Government Printing Office, 1977c), 61.

149. *U.S. v. Board of Education, Independent School District No. 1, Tulsa County, Oklahoma*, 459 F.2d 720 (10th Cir. 1972), at 724.

150. *U.S. v. Board of Education, Independent School District No. 1, Tulsa County, Oklahoma*, 476 F.2d 621 (10th Cir. 1973).

151. *U.S. v. Board of Education, Independent School District No. 1, Tulsa County, Oklahoma*, U.S. District Court, N.D. Okla., November 9, 1983. (Order Closing Case) No. 68-C-185-D.

Chapter 4

Comparing Different Types of School Desegregation Plans

HYPOTHESIS

Despite Rossell's (1990a, 1990b, 1988), and Rossell and Clarke's (1987) assertion that voluntary plans are more successful at desegregating school districts, the following hypothesis is proposed in order to test empirically the continuum designed in Chapter 3 (refer back to the latter section of this chapter for the categorization scheme and ensuing assignment rules): "HYP: Among school districts that have implemented desegregation plans, the greater the level of coercion utilized, the more desegregated the school system." This general hypothesis essentially operationalizes Hochschild's (1984: 71) assertion that "voluntary methods do not desegregate school districts."

In summary, it is hypothesized that segregation as measured by the Index of Dissimilarity will decrease by the greatest increments with the implementation of more coercive plans. Thus, the greatest reduction in segregation is hypothesized to occur at the far right-hand side of the continuum and then decrease as one moves from right to left.

DATA COLLECTION

In order to calculate the Index of Dissimilarity (D), one must obtain the racial breakdown by school within the district. Such data for a time-series of this magnitude are not always easily obtained. This is largely due to the fact that there is not a single, centralized source for such information—unless the local district involved has maintained an ongoing data base. In many cases, data are obtained from more than one source. The Office for Civil Rights conducted annual surveys of the racial/ethnic composition of pupils and full-time classroom teachers from 1967–68 through 1974–75. After 1974, however, the surveys were only administered in even years (i.e., 1976, 1978, 1980, and so on). Thus, the federal government is not a centralized source for racial/ethnic data at the local level, because of the critical missing years in a time-series analysis.

The primary source is at the local level. Administrators for the school districts complete surveys for the federal government. The ethnic categories are specified by the OCR. The districts are instructed to include a pupil in the group that he or she appears to belong, identifies with, or is regarded in the community as belonging to—no person is counted in more than one racial/ethnic category. The manner of collecting the information is left to the discretion of the school district, provided that its system results in reasonably accurate data. There are six categories as of 1988–89:

American Indian: A person having origins in any of the original peoples of North America and who maintains cultural identification through tribal affiliation or community recognition.

Black: (Not of Spanish origin). A person having origins in any of the black racial groups of Africa.

Asian or Pacific Islander: A person having origins in any of the original peoples of the Far East, Southeast Asia, the Pacific Islands, or the Indian subcontinent. This area includes, for example: China, India, Japan, Korea, the Philippine Islands, and Samoa.

Spanish: A person of Mexican, Puerto Rican, Cuban, Central or South American, or other Spanish culture or origin—regardless of race.

White: (Not of Spanish origin). A person having origins in any of the original peoples of Europe, North Africa, or the Middle East.

Other: A person not identifying with any of the above categories.

So, regardless of where the data are obtained, whether from OCR or from a state education department, the local districts are the original data source. Researchers may be fortunate enough to obtain a complete time-series directly from the school districts. If this is not the case, OCR data are available in tape format or in directories for selected years (1967, 1968, 1970, 1972, 1976, and 1978). Lastly, some states centralize local racial/ethnic data in their state education departments. Such was the case in Kentucky, New York, Oregon, and Texas in this sample. Scatter plots of the level of segregation as measured by the Index of Dissimilarity in each of the districts are located in the appendix to this chapter. Bear in mind that the higher the D score, the more segregated the district (i.e., 100 = perfect racial imbalance—all schools are one-race schools; 0 = perfect racial balance—all schools in the system reflect the same racial proportion as the district as a whole).

RESEARCH DESIGN

In order to address the research question (which type of school desegregation intervention facilitates the reduction of the level of segregation in the public schools best?), simple interrupted time-series analysis (SITS) and multiple interrupted time-series analysis (MITS) are employed. SITS is the most basic time-series design, and requires one experimental group and multiple pretest and posttest observations before and after a single treatment or intervention. Cook and Campbell (1979: 209) diagram this design in the following fashion:

---

01 02 03 04 05 × 06 07 08 09 010

SITS is utilized in those districts with a single major intervention designed for desegregation. This includes sixteen of the twenty school districts in the study:

SITS Analysis

Boston	Milwaukee	Springfield
Buffalo	Montgomery County	Stockton
Cincinnati	Racine	Tacoma
Dayton	St. Paul	Tulsa
Des Moines	San Bernardino	
Jefferson County	San Diego	

MITS analysis, on the other hand, involves multiple treatments or interventions. This type of design can be diagrammed as follows:

---

01 02 03 ×1 04 05 06 ×2 07 08 09 010

MITS is utilized in the four districts that implemented two distinct interventions:

MITS Analysis

Dallas
Houston
Montclair
Portland

According to Lewis-Beck and Alford (1980: 747), "Whenever one wishes to assess the impact of repeated policy changes over time, MITS analysis seems the preferred strategy." They analyze three major pieces of legislation designed to improve coal mining safety to substantiate their assertion.

The units of analysis in this evaluation are time points within the twenty districts under scrutiny. The time period of the study varies slightly depending upon the district. The earliest year in the time-series is the 1962–63 academic year in Tacoma. The time-series for the majority of the districts, however, commences in the mid- to late 1960s through 1988–89 for all the districts.

By What Criterion?

Before analyzing the regression results, an assessment of which type of intervention strategy most successfully desegregates the public schools will now be made. Since it is hypothesized that the most coercive types of plans desegregate school districts best, the lowest *D* values should be on the far right side of the continuum constructed in Chapter 3, and should increase from right to left by intervention type.

Three rigid criteria are presented in Table 4.1 to address the research question at hand. The results of the table indicate that the main hypothesis (that the most coercive types of plans desegregate the districts best), is supported, but only partially. The High Level of Coercion category is the least segregated under criterion #1 (during the last year of implementation); results in the largest decline in segregation under criterion #2 (between the first year before implementation and last year of implementation); and is the least segregated under criterion #3 (during the 1988–89 school year). The third criterion truly assists in substantiating the results of the first two, because it is often assumed that high levels of resegregation occur after desegregation in coercive plans, due to so-called "white flight." Thus, the most coercive intervention strategy on this continuum desegregated the schools most comprehensively under all three criteria.

The Moderate Level of Choice with Low Level of Coercion category, however, rated second best in two of the three criteria (#2 and #3). This does not support the hypothesis that the more coercive techniques utilized in the districts in the Moderate Level of Coercion with Low Level of Choice category will be more desegregated. This may be due to the fact that the level of segregation in Dallas, Houston, and Tulsa was over 90 on the *D* scale in the first year of available

Table 4.1

Means Analysis of Actual Index of Dissimilarity (*D*) Scores After Implementation of Desegregation Plans

CRITERION #1: Level of Segregation as Measured by the Index of Dissimilarity During Last Year of Implementation

Category	Mean of $\underline{D}$	Standard Deviation
High Level of Coercion (N=8)	28.7	6.7
Moderate Level of Coercion with Low Level of Choice (N=6)	60.8	25.2
Moderate Level of Choice with Low Level of Coercion (N=7)	48.8	21.5
High Level of Choice (N=3)	33.2*	21.8

*This figure is deceptively low, because Montclair was highly desegregated before implementation of the second plan ($\underline{D}$=13.2). Without Montclair II, the mean of the category is 45.8.

CRITERION #2: Drop in Segregation as Measured by the Index of Dissimilarity Between First Year Before Implementation and Last Year of Implementation

Category	Mean Drop in $\underline{D}$	Standard Deviation
High Level of Coercion (N=8)	-28.7	19.6
Moderate Level of Coercion with Low Level of Choice (N=6)	-12.6	6.5
Moderate Level of Choice with Low Level of Coercion (N=7)	-14.3	19.3
High Level of Choice (N=3)	- 9.8**	4.1

**Without Montclair II, the mean for this category is -12.2.

CRITERION #3: Level of Segregation as Measured by the Index of Dissimilarity in Most Recent Year of Data (1988-89 School Year) (Multiple intervention cities are omitted if more than one type of intervention strategy is involved)

Category	Mean of $\underline{D}$	Standard Deviation
High Level of Coercion (N=7)	26.5	9.4
Moderate Level of Coercion with Low Level of Choice (N=4)	42.5	21.5
Moderate Level of Choice with Low Level of Coercion (N=5)	34.0	14.8
High Level of Choice (N=2)	34.2	14.1

data (the only other district where this occurred was Dayton). Perhaps the plans did not entail enough schools or stringent enough racial composition goals to have a significantly larger impact on reducing the extremely high segregation levels. Or perhaps if even more coercive techniques had been utilized, these districts could have achieved less segregated schools.

Unfortunately for voluntary desegregation enthusiasts, the High Level of Choice category ranks second best under the first criterion, only third best under the third, and last in the second criterion. Note that Montclair is dropped from the analysis because it was highly desegregated comparatively speaking to begin with (under criterion #1), and thus had less leeway for a drop in D (under criterion #2). An examination of Smw in this same context is most illuminating, and may serve to highlight the discussion in Chapter 2.

Smw: Does the Measure Affect the Outcome?

A means analysis utilizing the same three criteria in Table 4.1 is presented in Table 4.2. The ultimate dependent variable is Smw, the proportion of white students in the average minority child's school. Utilization of Smw in this manner assists in the determination of whether or not one type of measure accounts for differences in the effectiveness of the interventions as opposed to another. Unlike D, the higher the Smw scores, the more desegregated the school district (i.e., more whites are in contact with minorities). The means test is conducted on two levels. The first utilizes the raw Smw scores; the second attempts to hold differential demographics constant across districts. The Smw score is divided by the percentage of white students in the district, which results in the proportion of whites who are exposed to minorities and may be a more meaningful basis for comparison.

When examining raw Smw scores under criterion #1, the High Level of Choice and High Level of Coercion categories fared the best—56.9 and 55.2 percent of whites were in contact with minorities, respectively. The Moderate Level of Coercion and Moderate Level of Choice categories lagged behind—44.2 percent and 42.9 percent, respectively. Under this criterion, the fringe categories on the continuum fared better, whether voluntary or coercive techniques were implemented.

The largest mean increase in Smw under criterion #2 is in the High Level of Coercion category (12.1 percent). The lowest is

Table 4.2
Means Analysis of Actual Interracial Exposure Index (*Smw*) Scores After Implementation of Desegregation Plans

Raw Smw Scores

CRITERION #1: Level of Interracial Exposure as Measured by the Interracial Exposure Index During Last Year of Implementation

Category	Mean of Smw	Standard Deviation
High Level of Coercion (N=8)	.552	.173
Moderate Level of Coercion with Low Level of Choice (N=6)	.442	.284
Moderate Level of Choice with Low Level of Coercion (N=7)	.429	.184
High Level of Choice (N=3)	.569	.146

CRITERION #2: Increase in Interracial Exposure as Measured by the Interracial Exposure Index Between First Year Before Implementation and Last Year of Implementation

Category	Mean Increase in Smw	Standard Deviation
High Level of Coercion (N=8)	.121	.150
Moderate Level of Coercion with Low Level of Choice (N=6)	.071	.059
Moderate Level of Choice with Low Level of Coercion (N=7)	.056	.072
High Level of Choice (N=3)	.023	.049

CRITERION #3: Level of Interracial Exposure as Measured by the Interracial Exposure Index in Most Recent Year of Data (1988-89 School Year)
(Multiple intervention cities are omitted if more than one type of intervention strategy is involved)

Category	Mean of Smw	Standard Deviation
High Level of Coercion (N=7)	.422	.187
Moderate Level of Coercion with Low Level of Choice (N=4)	.505	.271
Moderate Level of Choice with Low Level of Coercion (N=5)	.393	.127
High Level of Choice (N=2)	.499	.223

Table 4.2 (continued)

Smw Scores Divided by % White in District

CRITERION #1: Level of Interracial Exposure as Measured by the
Interracial Exposure Index During Last Year of Implementation

Category	Mean of Smw	Standard Deviation
High Level of Coercion (N=8)	90.2	2.8
Moderate Level of Coercion with Low Level of Choice (N=6)	66.0	25.0
Moderate Level of Choice with Low Level of Coercion (N=7)	74.8	18.3
High Level of Choice (N=3)	86.6	10.7

CRITERION #2: Increase in Interracial Exposure as Measured by the
Interracial Exposure Index Between First Year Before
Implementation and Last Year of Implementation

Category	Mean Increase in Smw	Standard Deviation
High Level of Coercion (N=8)	27.5	20.8
Moderate Level of Coercion with Low Level of Choice (N=6)	14.3	6.0
Moderate Level of Choice with Low Level of Coercion (N=7)	15.3	16.4
High Level of Choice (N=3)	7.5	5.2

CRITERION #3: Level of Interracial Exposure as Measured by the
Interracial Exposure Index in Most Recent Year of Data (1988-89
School Year)
(Multiple intervention cities are omitted if more than one type
of intervention strategy is involved)

Category	Mean of Smw	Standard Deviation
High Level of Coercion (N=7)	92.0	4.6
Moderate Level of Coercion with Low Level of Choice (N=4)	83.9	12.7
Moderate Level of Choice with Low Level of Coercion (N=5)	87.2	7.0
High Level of Choice (N=2)	88.5	8.6

---

in the High Level of Choice category (2.3 percent). These results, however, may be tainted, due to the large standard deviations. The mean of *Smw* in 1988–89 is highest in the Moderate Level of Coercion category (50.5 percent), and in descending order: High Level of Choice (49.9 percent), High Level of Coercion (42.4 percent), and Moderate Level of Choice (39.3 percent).

When standardizing the scores for comparative purposes by dividing *Smw* by the district's proportion of white students, similar results are generated under criterion #1 above. The fringe categories of High Level of Coercion and High Level of Choice fared better—90.2 percent and 86.6 percent, respectively, compared to 74.8 percent (Moderate Level of Choice) and 66 percent (Moderate Level of Coercion).

Again, similar to criterion #2 above, the High Level of Coercion category increased *Smw* by the most (27.5 percent) and the High Level of Choice category the least (7.5 percent). Results under the third criterion differ, however. The mean of the High Level of Coercion category is 92 percent to 88.5 percent (High Level of Choice), 87.2 percent (Moderate Level of Choice), and 83.9 percent (Moderate Level of Coercion).

One point quite clearly stands out in Table 4.2. When standardizing *Smw* for a more meaningful basis of comparison, the High Level of Coercion category fares the best under all three criteria. Even without standardization, this type of intervention fared as well as the High Level of Choice category under criterion #1, and is at the top of the list under criterion #2. It does not compare as well as Moderate Level of Coercion or High Level of Choice under criterion #3. Thus, despite Rossell (1990a, 1990b, 1988), and Rossell and Clarke's (1987) determination that voluntarism is preferable to coercion, the results here would indicate otherwise. Regardless of whether *Smw* or *D* is utilized, the most coercive type of intervention brings more whites into contact with minorities and improves the racial balance of the schools to a greater extent. Given these findings and the theoretical and statistical propositions put forth in Chapter 2, it would seem implausible to utilize *Smw* as a measure of segregation in evaluations such as this. *D* is both conceptually and methodologically superior to *Smw*—even when *Smw* is used, the most coercive type of intervention is the most effective.

REGRESSION ANALYSIS

Ordinary Least Squares (OLS) regression is utilized to test the impact of the interventions on segregation in each of the districts. Three different equations are employed, depending upon the intervention strategy involved.

SITS Analysis

SITS analysis is utilized in sixteen of the districts. Yet the regression equations for each are not the same. Ordinary Least Squares regression assumes a general linear pattern for the data. This is the case in Cincinnati, Dayton, Des Moines, Jefferson County, Montgomery County, Racine, Springfield, Tacoma, and Tulsa. Thus, in order to test the impact of the intervention on segregation, the optimum equation for these districts is:

$$D = a + b_1 \text{(Time)} + b_2 \text{(Intervention)} + b_3 \text{(Time} \times \text{Intervention)} + e,$$

where

D = Index of Dissimilarity

Time = Counter for years (1 to N)

Intervention = Dichotomous variable (0 = before intervention; 1 = implementation of intervention and after)

Time × Intervention = Interaction between time and the intervention (0 = before intervention; 1,2,3 . . . = implementation of intervention and after)

e = Error term

These variables are scaled similarly to those utilized in Lewis-Beck and Alford's (1980) "coal mine example."

The data for the other districts in this design category does not demonstrate a linear pattern after implementation of the intervention. While some of the districts above employed a phase-in strategy (Cincinnati, Springfield, and Tulsa), Boston, Buffalo, Milwaukee, St. Paul, San Bernardino, San Diego, and Stockton all did so and demonstrate a curvilinear trend during their respective periods. If Y (the Index of Dissimilarity) decreases nonlinearly as X (time in years) increases, then the model becomes a reciprocal transformation (Gujarati, 1988: 150–52). Models of this type are captured in this fashion:

$$Y = a + b_1 + b_2 (1/X) + e$$

Thus, the equation for these districts becomes:

$$D = a + b_1 (\text{Time}) + b_2 (\text{Intervention}) + b_3 (\text{Phase-in}) + e,$$

where

D = Index of Dissimilarity

Time = Counter for years (1 to N)

Intervention = Dichotomous variable (0 = before intervention; 1 = implementation of intervention and after)

Phase-in = Interaction between time and the intervention (0 = before intervention; becomes a reciprocal transformation after this:

$1/1 = 1$ First year of implementation

$1/2 = .50$ Second year of implementation

$1/3 = .33$ Third year of implementation

$1/4 = .25$ Fourth year of implementation

And so on depending upon the length of the phase-in period in the district After the phase-in is complete, the time period continues sequentially. In this example, after the fourth and final year of the phase-in, the variable is scaled 5,6,7 . . .)

e = Error term

MITS Analysis

The optimum equation for those districts that implemented two distinct desegregation plans follows the same pattern as those introduced above, yet requires slightly more information:

$$D = a + b_1 \text{(Time)} + b_2 \text{(Intervention #1)} +$$
$$b_3 \text{(Time} \times \text{Intervention #1)} + b_4 \text{(Intervention #2)} +$$
$$b_5 \text{(Time} \times \text{Intervention #2)} + e,$$

where

D = Index of Dissimilarity

Time = Counter for years (1 to N)

Intervention #1 = Dichotomous variable (0 = before first intervention; 1 = implementation of first intervention and after)

Time × Intervention #1 = Interaction between time and the first intervention (Scaled 0 = before intervention; 1,2,3 . . . = implementation of first intervention and after)

Intervention #2 = Dichotomous variable (0 = before second intervention; 1 = implementation of second intervention and after)

Time × Intervention #2 = Interaction between time and the second intervention (Scaled 0 = before intervention; 1,2,3 . . . = implementation of second intervention and after)

e = Error term

Table 4.3
Regression Results

	SITS Analysis			

Dependent Variable: Index of Dissimilarity (D)

	Boston	Buffalo	Cincinnati	Dayton	Des Moines
Intercept	74.7	77.7	66.1	93.1	69.8
		Slope Values			
Time	-.19	-2.0*	.33	-2.6**	-1.6**
	(.85)	(.73)	(.29)	(.24)	(.24)
Intervention	-40.2**	-16.8*	4.2**	-46.2**	-10.2**
	(5.1)	(6.3)	(1.3)	(1.6)	(1.9)
Time* Intervention	------	------	-2.5**	2.3**	1.1**
			(.30)	(.27)	(.30)
Phase-in	.33	-.35	------	------	------
	(.77)	(.63)			

Note: Standard errors are in parentheses.
    * = significant at .05 level (2-tail).
   ** = significant at .01 level (2-tail).

These variables, again, are scaled similarly to those utilized in Lewis-Beck and Alford (1980).

INTERPRETATION OF RESULTS

The results of the regression analysis are available in Table 4.3. Interpretation of these results lends greater understanding of the desegregation process in each of the districts. The reader may wish to refer back to the scatter plots in the appendix to this chapter while doing so. It is also helpful at this time to determine the levels of segregation for each category for the first year of available data.

Table 4.3 (continued)

SITS Analysis

<u>Dependent Variable</u>: Index of Dissimilarity (<u>D</u>)

	Jefferson County	Milwaukee	Montgomery County	Racine	St Paul
Intercept	80.5	88.7	67.0	68.6	73.0

Slope Values

	Jefferson County	Milwaukee	Montgomery County	Racine	St Paul
Time	.18 (.26)	-1.2** (.42)	-3.0** (.18)	-2.8** (.21)	-1.4** (.39)
Intervention	-57.2** (1.5)	-33.1** (3.0)	.55 (1.5)	-24.9** (1.2)	-9.4** (2.9)
Time* Intervention	-.89** (.29)	------	3.2** (.23)	2.2** (.23)	------
Phase-in	------	-.18 (.43)	------	------	.28 (.40)

Note: Standard errors are in parentheses.
    * = significant at .05 level (2-tail).
  ** = significant at .01 level (2-tail).

Table 4.4 is a means analysis of actual intercept values by intervention type. The table indicates that the mean of *D* in each category is extremely high (between 70 and 80) and very similar. This indicates that the majority of these districts were very segregated in the mid- to late 1960s, so that one intervention type is not at a comparative disadvantage to the others, because they all started at relatively similar levels of segregation.

Boston

The intercept is where the predicted value of *Y* intersects with the *Y* axis. In the case of Boston, this occurs in the 1967–68 school year, or the first year of available data. The intercept value means

Table 4.3 (continued)

	SITS Analysis					
Dependent Variable: Index of Dissimilarity (D)						
	San Bernardino	San Diego	Springfield	Stockton	Tacoma	Tulsa
Intercept	56.7	85.8	58.0	81.7	71.3	93.3
	Slope Values					
Time	-2.0**	-2.2**	-2.4**	-1.8**	-2.3**	-2.6**
	(.26)	(.16)	(.45)	(.53)	(.53)	(.74)
Intervention	-6.4**	-5.0**	-14.2**	-23.3**	-18.6**	-4.7**
	(2.1)	(1.6)	(2.8)	(4.9)	(2.0)	(1.6)
Time* Intervention	------	------	2.3**	------	1.6**	1.1
			(.49)		(.53)	(.75)
Phase-in	1.1**	1.1**	------	.61	------	------
	(.30)	(.18)		(.47)		

Note: Standard errors are in parentheses.
    * = significant at .05 level (2-tail).
    ** = significant at .01 level (2-tail).

that the Boston public schools had a *D* score of 74.7 at this time. The time variable is not significantly different from zero, meaning that segregation did not demonstrate a systematic pattern of decline until the intervention. Upon implementation of the intervention, *D* decreased by 40.2 during Phase I, meaning that the district was much less segregated than before the desegregation plan. Within the High Level of Coercion category, Boston ranks third in overall decrease in segregation as a result of the intervention. In fact, this category includes the three largest decreases in segregation as a result of the intervention compared to the other three intervention types (Jefferson County, Dayton, and Boston). The phase-in variable is also not significantly different from zero,

Table 4.3 (continued)

	D a l l a s	H o u s t o n	M o n t c l a i r	P o r t l a n d
MITS Analysis				
Dependent Variable: Index of Dissimilarity (D)				
Intercept	93.4	91.0	35.0	73.3
Slope Values				
Time	.40 (.91)	.05 (.48)	-1.2 (1.0)	-1.6* (.61)
Intervention#1	-11.3** (1.8)	-5.9** (.95)	-8.7** (2.9)	.84 (2.6)
Time* Intervention#1	-1.9 (1.0)	-1.3* (.53)	-.40 (1.2)	-.79 (.68)
Intervention#2	-12.1** (1.3)	-.51 (.65)	-3.3 (2.2)	8.8** (2.4)
Time* Intervention#2	1.4** (.42)	.12 (.22)	1.2 (.58)	3.2** (.44)

Note: Standard errors are in parentheses.
* = significant at .05 level (2-tail).
** = significant at .01 level (2-tail).

indicating that it had no systematic pattern of decline similar to the time variable.

Buffalo

The Buffalo public schools had a *D* score of 77.7 in 1967. The slope value of the time variable is -2.0, indicating that *D* decreased by two points every year until the intervention. *D* decreased by 16.8 upon initial implementation of the intervention. This ranks Buffalo just behind Milwaukee in the Moderate Level of Choice with Low Level of Coercion category in terms of the most desegregation as a result of the intervention. The phase-in variable resulted in no systematic pattern of decline in segregation.

Table 4.4
Means Analysis of Actual Intercept Values by Category

Category	Mean of $\underline{D}$	Standard Deviation
High Level of Coercion (N=7)	75.0	9.2
Moderate Level of Coercion with Low Level of Choice (N=4)	79.7	14.8
Moderate Level of Choice with Low Level of Coercion (N=5)	71.8	9.5
High Level of Choice (N=2)	75.9	9.5

Note: Multiple intervention cities are omitted if more than one type of intervention strategy is involved.

Cincinnati

In 1966, the Cincinnati public schools had a *D* score of 66.1. The time variable is not statistically different from zero, indicating that the segregation trend did not show a systematic pattern of decline until the intervention. The slope coefficient for the intervention variable is positive, indicating that the desegregation plan actually increased *D* (by 4.2). This is evidence of a very unsuccessful plan, because a desegregation order is designed to reduce segregation. Indeed, the Cincinnati plan ranked only better than the second Portland plan in the Moderate Level of Choice with Low Level of Coercion category in reducing segregation. The interaction term is the cumulative slope change when the time variable is factored in—thus, -2.5 plus .33 is equal to -2.17. This simply means that *D* decreased by 2.17 every year after the intervention was implemented.

Dallas

The Dallas Independent School District had a *D* score of 93.4 in 1968. At that time in Dallas, almost every school was uniracial, in violation of the mandate of *Brown I*. The time variable is not significantly different from zero, and no systematic pattern of decline is witnessed until implementation of the first intervention.

The first major desegregation plan decreased D by 11.3. The interaction term between time and the first intervention is also not statistically significant. The second plan decreased D by 12.1, while the interaction term between time and the second intervention is the cumulative slope change when time and the interaction between time and the first intervention are factored in—1.4 plus .40 plus -1.9 is equal to -.1. D decreased by .1 every year after implementation of the second desegregation plan. Within the Moderate Level of Coercion with Low Level of Choice category, the second intervention ranks second to Racine in the most reduction in D, and the first intervention is third overall.

Dayton

In 1967, the Dayton public schools scored 93.1 on the D scale. Like Dallas, most schools were uniracial at that time. D decreased by 2.6 every year until implementation of the major plan in 1976. This plan resulted in a decrease in D by 46.2, which is the second largest decrease among any type of plan (second only to Jefferson County). Again, both Dayton and Jefferson County belong in the High Level of Coercion category. The interaction term of 2.3 with the slope coefficient of -2.6 factored in results in a decrease in D by .3 every year after the intervention.

Des Moines

The Des Moines Independent Community School District had a D score of 69.8 in 1967. It was not as segregated as Dallas, Houston, and Tulsa, which all utilized the same type of intervention (these three districts had intercepts > 90). This score decreased by 1.6 every year until the intervention. The major plan resulted in a further decline in D by 10.2, which ranks Des Moines fourth best in the Moderate Level of Coercion with Low Level of Choice category in terms of reducing segregation. The interaction term of 1.1 plus the slope of time (-1.6) resulted in a net decline in D by a modest .5 every year after the intervention.

Houston

In 1967, the Houston Independent School District had a D score of 91. The time trend does not indicate a systematic pattern of decline until the first intervention. The first major plan in 1970 resulted in a net decline in D of 5.9. This intervention type is classified in the Moderate Level of Coercion with Low Level of Choice category and ranks only fifth (of six) in terms of largest reduction in D. The interaction between time and this first intervention is equal to -1.3. Therefore, D decreased by 1.25 after implementation of the first plan until the second one went into effect (-1.3 plus the slope of the time variable, .05). The coefficient for the second intervention is equal to -.51, but it is not significantly different from zero, meaning that it had no true impact on the level of segregation. Although the impact of this second plan is virtually negligible, it ranked better than the Cincinnati plan and the second Portland plan in the Moderate Level of Choice with Low Level of Coercion category because those interventions actually increased segregation. The second interaction term is also not reflective of a systematic pattern of decline in segregation.

Jefferson County

In 1967, the Jefferson County public schools had a D score of 80.5. Segregation did not systematically decline until the intervention, as the time variable is not significant. The intervention resulted in a decrease in D by 57.2. As previously mentioned, this is the largest decrease of any intervention of the twenty-four desegregation efforts under scrutiny and belongs in the High Level of Coercion category. The interaction term is the cumulative slope change when time is factored in— -.89 plus .18 is equal to -.71. D decreased by .71 every year after the intervention was implemented.

Milwaukee

The Milwaukee public schools' D score was 88.7 in 1967, indicating that it was highly segregated at that time. The time variable indicates that D decreased by 1.2 every year until the major plan. Implementation of the intervention caused D to decrease by 33.1. This plan resulted in the greatest decline in segregation after initial implementation in the Moderate Level of Choice with Low Level of Coercion category. The phase-in variable is not significant, indicating that it had no systematic impact on the level of segregation.

Montclair

The smallest district in the sample, the Montclair public schools, also had the lowest D score in the first year of available data. In 1967, this score was a modest 35. The time coefficent did not show a systematic pattern of decline until the first intervention. The first intervention, however, did systematically reduce D by 8.7. This plan belongs in the High Level of Coercion category, but ranks only better than Montgomery County, which has a positive coefficient (of the eight interventions in this division). The slope coefficient for the second intervention is equal to -3.3 but is not significantly different from zero, indicating that it had no true systematic impact on D. The intervention coefficients for the other two plans in the High Level of Choice category demonstrate a greater impact on segregation (-18.6 in Tacoma and -5.0 in San Diego). Neither interaction term resulted in a systematic pattern of decline in segregation.

Montgomery County

Montgomery County's D score was 67 in 1965. Time is very important in this equation, as it reduced D by 3 each year until the intervention. The intervention, however, is equal to .55 and is not significant, meaning that it had no systematic impact on the level of segregation in the schools. This plan is the least successful of the eight classified in the High Level of Coercion category and is also the only positive coefficient. The interaction term is equal to 3.2, so the cumulative change in *D* with the time coefficient factored in is .2. *D* increased by this amount each year after the intervention.

Portland

The intercept for the Portland public schools was 73.3 in 1964. *D* decreased by 1.6 every year until the first intervention. The coefficient for the first plan is .84 and is not statistically significant, indicating that it had no impact on *D*. The interaction between time and the first plan is also not indicative of a systematic decline in segregation. The second intervention is significant, however, but the coefficient is positive (8.8). It had the effect of increasing segregation in the school system by 8.8 on the *D* scale. This makes the second Portland plan not only the least successful of the plans in the Moderate Level of Choice with Low Level of Coercion category, but among all the desegregation plans in this study, as well. The first plan only fared better than Cincinnati and the second plan in its intervention type. The interaction term between time and the second intervention is the cumulative slope change when time and the interaction between time and the first intervention are factored in—thus, 3.2 plus -1.6 plus -.79 is equal to .81. *D* increased by .81 each year after implementation of the second intervention.

Racine

The Racine Unified School District had a *D* score of 68.6 in 1967. *D* decreased by 2.8 each year until implementation of the major plan. The intervention resulted in a decrease of 24.9 in *D*, making Racine the most successful district in the Moderate Level of Coercion with Low Level of Choice category in reducing segregation. The interaction term is equal to 2.2; with time factored in the cumulative slope change equals -.6. D decreased by this increment each year following the intervention.

St. Paul

The St. Paul public schools were segregated to the extent of a 73 on the D scale in 1964. The slope coefficient for time indicates that D decreased by 1.4 each year until the intervention. The intervention caused D to decrease by 9.4, a modest decline when compared to other districts in the High Level of Coercion category (sixth of eight plans), while the phase-in variable did not result in a systematic pattern of decline in segregation.

San Bernardino

In 1968, the San Bernardino City Unified School District's Index of Dissimilarity score was 56.7. The slope of time indicates that D decreased by 2 each year until the intervention. The major plan resulted in a further decline in D by 6.4 in the first year of implementation, ranking it behind Milwaukee and Buffalo in the Moderate Level of Choice with Low Level of Coercion category. The phase-in variable is statistically significant (slope = 1.1), and because the variable is scaled in both fractions because of the reciprocal transformation and sequential time, is indicative of a downward curvilinear slope during the phase-in period (1978–80) and a slight increase afterwards.

San Diego

The San Diego Unified School District had a D score of 85.8 in 1965, the highest intercept among the districts in the High Level of Choice category. The slope coefficient for the time variable indicates that D decreased by 2.2 each year until implementation of the intervention. D decreased by 5 with the intervention, and the slope for the phase-in variable is equal to 1.1, as was also the case of San Bernardino. There was a downward curvilinear slope during the phase-in period (1977–80) and a slight increase afterwards in D. The intervention in San Diego was slightly more successful than the second plan in Montclair, and less successful than the one in Tacoma among those represented in the High Level of Choice category.

Springfield

In 1965, the Springfield public schools had a D score of 58. The slope for the time variable indicates that the level of segregation decreased by 2.4 each year until the intervention. The major plan resulted in a decrease in D of 14.2, and the interaction term is equal to 2.3, meaning that when time is factored in, D decreased by .1 each year after the intervention. The decline as a result of the intervention ranks Springfield fifth (out of eight) in the High Level of Coercion category.

Stockton

The Stockton Unified School District had a D score of 81.7 in 1965. Time resulted in a decrease in D by 1.8 each year until implementation of the major plan. Implementation caused a 23.3 decrease in D, ranking it just ahead of Springfield in the High Level of Coercion category. The phase-in variable did not result in a systematic pattern of decline in D.

Tacoma

The Tacoma public schools' D score was 71.3 in 1962. The time variable is statistically significant, and resulted in a yearly decrease in D by 2.3, while the intervention lowered D by an additional 18.6. This is the largest decline in segregation among the three districts in the High Level of Choice category. The slope of the interaction term (1.6), when coupled with the slope change in the time variable (-2.3), resulted in a net change in D of -.7 every year after implementation of the desegregation plan.

Tulsa

The Tulsa public schools in 1967 had a *D* score of 93.3, making it one of three districts with an intercept of > 90 in the Moderate Level of Coercion with Low Level of Choice category (the other two are Dallas and Houston). The index decreased by 2.6 each year until the intervention. Upon implementation of the major plan, *D* decreased by 4.7, which is the smallest decline of the six districts in its category. The slope of the interaction term is not statistically significant, and does not demonstrate a systematic pattern of decline in segregation.

CONCLUSION

The analysis demonstrates that the most coercive desegregation techniques desegregate school districts best. The second most coercive type of intervention strategy did not desegregate the districts to the extent hypothesized. Yet as discussed above, this may be attributable to an overrepresentation of extremely segregated districts in this category. The Moderate Level of Choice with Low Level of Coercion category ranked behind the High Level of Coercion category in reducing segregation. This reduction in segregation is due to the successful desegregation efforts in Buffalo, Milwaukee, and San Bernardino, and not the cases of Cincinnati, both interventions in Portland, and the second intervention in Houston. Lastly, the data show that efforts falling in the High Level of Choice category, when the second Montclair intervention is omitted, did not desegregate schools as well as the most coercive type of intervention (High Level of Coercion), or the third most coercive type of intervention (Moderate Level of Choice with Low Level of Coercion). It did, however, rank better than the second most coercive type (Moderate Level of Coercion with Low Level of Choice).

Although the results are slightly mixed, they do strongly point in one direction. The goal of desegregation is most successfully met when whites are coerced into desegregation by the school districts (which in turn may be pressured or directed to desegregate by external sources). If given the choice, whites will not choose to mix with other racial groups to the extent that they will when given very little choice. Given these findings, it now becomes very important to examine an issue that is inextricably linked to desegregation efforts—the phenomenon commonly referred to as "white flight" from desegregation.

**APPENDIX: SCATTER PLOTS OF THE LEVEL OF
SEGREGATION AS MEASURED BY THE INDEX OF
DISSIMILARITY IN EACH DISTRICT**

Boston, Massachusetts (Boston Public Schools)

Plot of Index of Dissimilarity Scores, 1967/68-1988/89

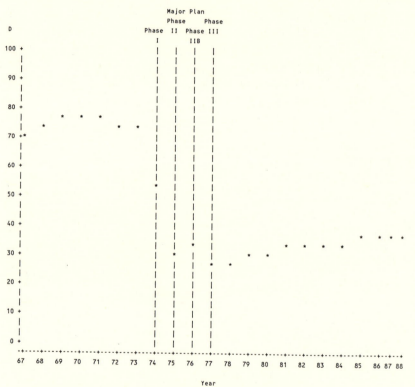

Buffalo, New York (Buffalo Public Schools)

Plot of Index of Dissimilarity Scores, 1967/68-1988/89

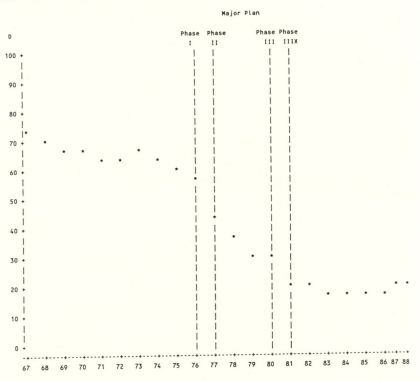

Cincinnati, Ohio (Cincinnati Public Schools)

Plot of Index of Dissimilarity Scores, 1966/67-1988/89

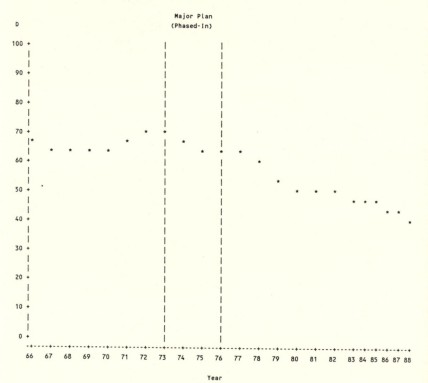

Dallas, Texas (Dallas Independent School District)

Plot of Index of Dissimilarity Scores, 1968/69-1988/89

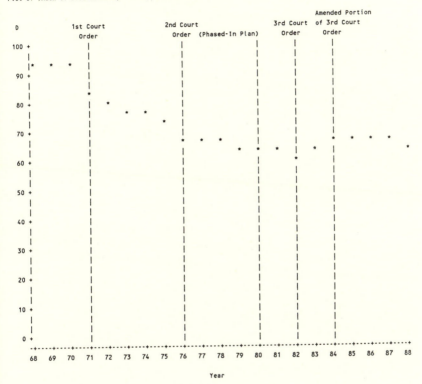

Year

Dayton, Ohio (Dayton Public Schools)

Plot of Index of Dissimilarity Scores, 1967/68-1988/89

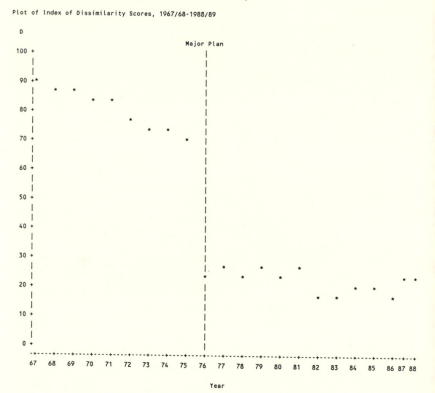

Des Moines, Iowa (Des Moines Independent Community School District)

Plot of Index of Dissimilarity Scores, 1967/68-1988/89

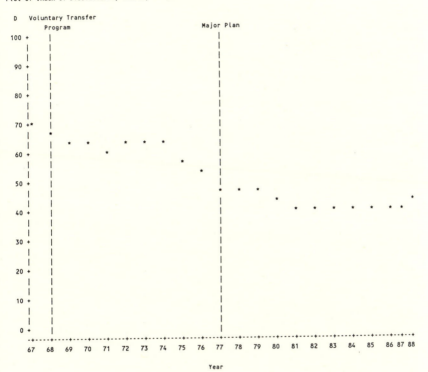

Year

Houston, Texas (Houston Independent School District)

Plot of Index of Dissimilarity Scores, 1967/68-1988/89

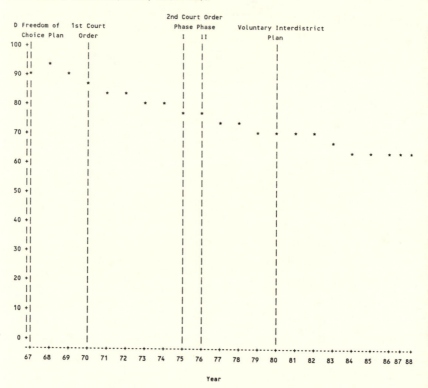

Year

Jefferson County/Louisville, Kentucky (Jefferson County Public Schools)

Plot of Index of Dissimilarity Scores, 1967/68-1988/89

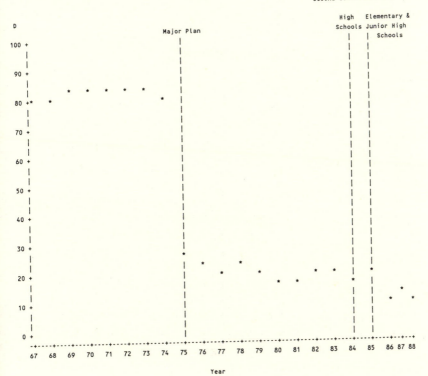

Milwaukee, Wisconsin (Milwaukee Public Schools)

Plot of Index of Dissimilarity Scores, 1967/68-1988/89

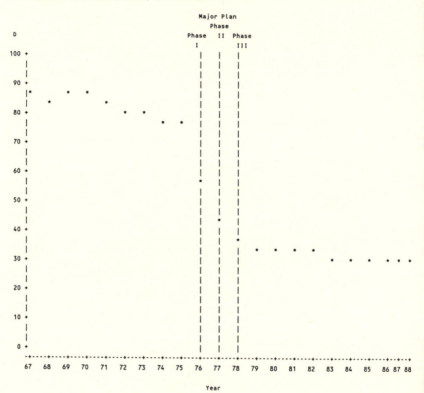

Montclair, New Jersey (Montclair Public Schools)

Plot of Index of Dissimilarity Scores, 1967/68-1988/89

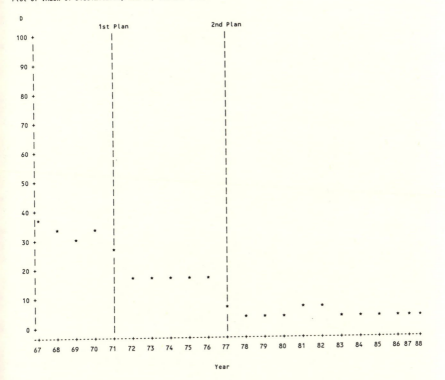

Montgomery County, Maryland (Montgomery County Public Schools)

Plot of Index of Dissimilarity Scores, 1965/66-1988/89

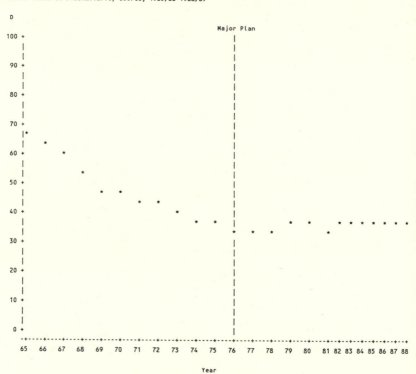

Portland, Oregon (Portland Public Schools)

Plot of Index of Dissimilarity Scores, 1964/65-1988/89

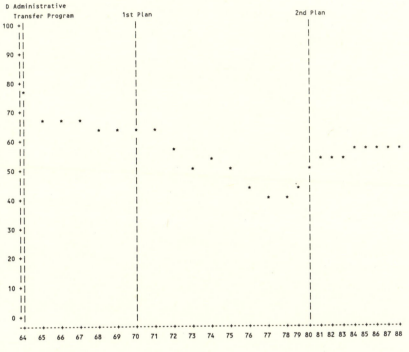

Racine, Wisconsin (Racine Unified School District)

Plot of Index of Dissimilarity Scores, 1967/68-1988/89

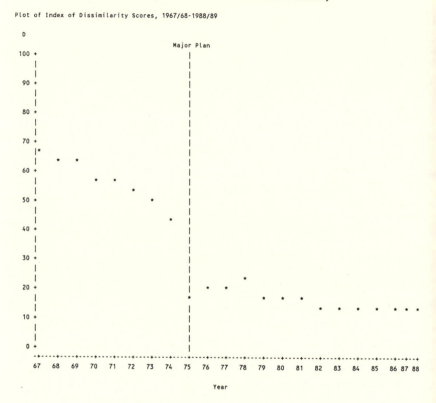

St. Paul, Minnesota (St. Paul Public Schools)

Plot of Index of Dissimilarity Scores, 1964/65-1988/89

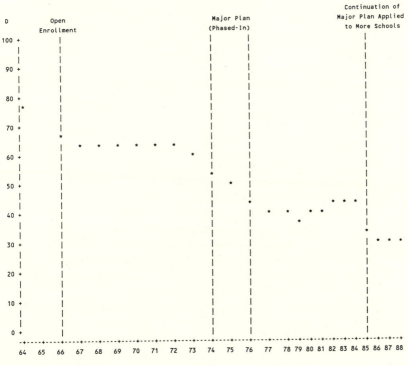

Year

San Bernardino, California (San Bernardino City Unified School District)

Plot of Index of Dissimilarity Scores, 1968/69-1988/89

```
 D        Redrawing of                          Major Plan
          Attendance Zones                      (Phased-In)
100 +          |                              |    |
    |          |                              |    |
    |          |                              |    |
 90 +          |                              |    |
    |          |                              |    |
    |          |                              |    |
 80 +          |                              |    |
    |          |                              |    |
    |          |                              |    |
 70 +          |                              |    |
    |          |                              |    |
    |          |                              |    |
 60 +*         |                              |    |
    |          |                              |    |
    |      *   |                              |    |
 50 +          *                              |    |
    |          |   *    *        *            |    |
  ⸱ |          |                              |    |
 40 +          |            *      *    *    *|    |
    |          |                       *      |    |
    |          |                              |    |
 30 +          |                              |    |
    |          |                         *   *|  *    *    *      *    *    *
    |          |                              |    |
 20 +          |                              |    |              *              *    *
    |          |                              |    |
    |          |                              |    |
 10 +          |                              |    |
    |          |                              |    |
    |          |                              |    |
  0 +          |                              |    |
   -+----+----+----+----+----+----+----+----+----+----+----+----+----+----+----+----+----+----+----+----+
    68   69   70   71   72   73   74   75   76   77   78   79   80   81   82   83   84   85   86   87   88

                                        Year
```

San Diego, California (San Diego Unified School District)

Plot of Index of Dissimilarity Scores, 1965/66-1988/89

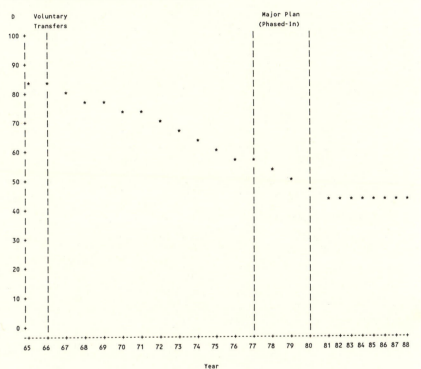

Year

Springfield, Massachusetts (Springfield Public Schools)

Plot of Index of Dissimilarity Scores, 1965/66-1988/89

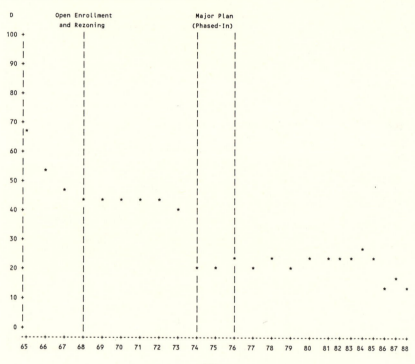

Year

Stockton, California (Stockton Unified School District)

Plot of Index of Dissimilarity Scores, 1965/66-1988/89

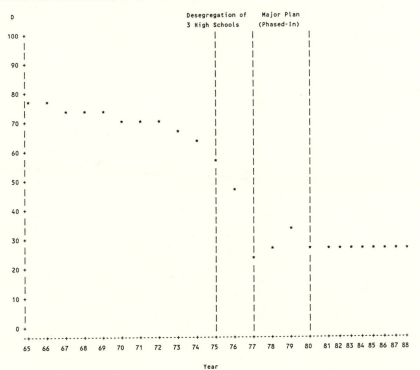

Year

Tacoma, Washington (Tacoma Public Schools)

Plot of Index of Dissimilarity Scores, 1962/63-1988/89

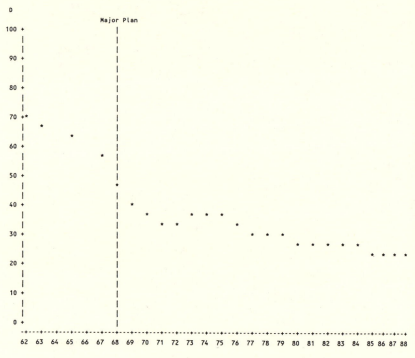

Tulsa, Oklahoma (Tulsa Public Schools)

Plot of Index of Dissimilarity Scores, 1967/68-1988/89

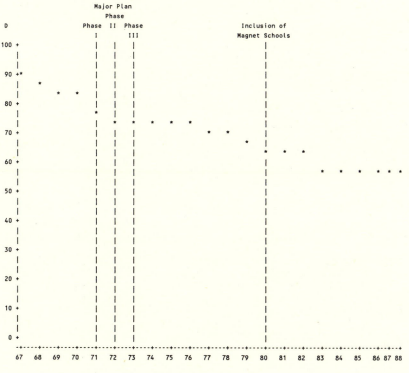

Year

Chapter 5

The "White Flight" Hypothesis Revisited

The purpose of this book is not to resolve the "white flight" issue, but to determine whether or not one type of school desegregation plan results in more white migration than another. The issue, in fact, is anything but resolved at the present time. While many researchers have concluded that school desegregation plans accelerate white migration from the public schools (e.g., Coleman, 1975; Bosco & Robin, 1976; Rossell, 1978; Farley, Richards, & Wurdock, 1980; Armor, 1980; Rossell, 1983; Smylie, 1983; and O'Grady, 1986), others have determined that white enrollment losses occur at roughly constant rates irrespective of intervention type (e.g., Farley, 1975; Rossell, 1975a, 1975b; Pettigrew & Green, 1976; Willie & Fultz, 1984). One point cannot be disputed, however. White student enrollment in urban public schools has dropped precipitously over the last two decades.

WHITE ENROLLMENT LOSSES IN URBAN AMERICA

That white public school enrollments in large urban cities have decreased over time is quite apparent. Table 5.1 compiles the proportionate change in white enrollment from T-1 to T. Data for each district ranges from the mid- to late 1960s through 1988-89 for all districts. Out of 431 school years, 396 showed a

Table 5.1

Percentage Change in White Enrollment from T-1 to T in Twenty School Districts

Year	Boston	Buffalo	Cincinnati	Dallas	Dayton	Des Moines	Houston	Jefferson County	Milwaukee	Montclair
1966	--	--	--	--	--	--	--	--	--	--
1967	--	--	-1.2	--	--	--	--	--	--	--
1968	-4.2	-2.5	-1.5	--	+5.4	0	-14.4	+0.1	-0.3	-1.5
1969	-2.5	-1.3	-0.3	-2.1	-1.1	0	-0.6	+0.4	-2.4	+2.3
1970	-1.9	-1.3	-1.7	-1.8	-1.4	-0.5	-3.3	+0.1	-0.3	-4.2
1971	-2.6	-1.1	-0.1	-3.4	-2.0	-0.1	-2.5	+0.4	-2.5	-1.1
1972	-1.9	-2.1	-2.3	-3.3	-2.0	-0.8	-2.8	-0.5	-1.7	-1.1
1973	-2.4	-2.4	-1.3	-3.3	-1.7	-0.4	-3.2	-0.5	-2.0	-0.9
1974	-4.8	-0.3	-1.5	-2.8	-1.2	-0.4	-2.4	-1.6	-2.5	-0.5
1975	-5.3	-0.8	-0.6	-3.2	-1.0	-0.9	-2.0	-1.5	-1.5	-1.6
1976	-3.1	-1.3	-2.1	-3.2	-3.8	-1.1	-2.5	-1.6	-3.8	+0.3
1977	-2.4	-1.4	-0.8	-2.6	-1.3	-1.4	-1.9	+0.1	-2.9	-1.1
1978	-2.0	-0.6	-1.7	-1.7	-1.2	-0.1	-2.7	-1.5	-2.8	-0.5
1979	-2.5	-1.2	-0.5	-1.6	-0.9	-1.0	-2.0	-0.5	-2.9	-0.4
1980	-1.9	-0.5	-1.1	-2.3	-0.7	-0.9	-2.2	-0.6	-2.4	-1.4
1981	-2.9	-0.4	+0.1	-2.2	-0.7	-0.9	-1.9	-1.0	-2.0	-2.0
1982	-2.5	-0.4	-0.2	-1.5	-0.6	-0.5	-1.6	-0.3	-1.5	+0.3
1983	-1.9	-0.4	0	-1.3	-0.9	+0.1	-1.4	-0.8	-1.8	-0.7
1984	-0.2	-0.5	-0.6	-1.4	-1.0	0	-1.3	-0.5	-2.1	+0.4
1985	-0.3	-0.8	-0.8	-1.9	-0.6	+0.3	-1.4	-1.4	-1.3	+0.4
1986	-1.5	-1.0	-1.8	-1.1	-1.4	-0.1	-0.7	+0.6	-1.4	-0.8
1987	-1.4	-0.7	-0.6	-0.4	-0.2	-0.4	-0.6	-0.6	-1.0	-1.2
1988	-1.2	-0.7	-1.0	-1.0	-0.8	0	-0.8	+0.5	-1.0	-0.1

decrease in the percentage of white enrollment. Twenty-seven years showed an increase, and in eight years there was no change in white enrollment percentage. Yet even if the percentage decrease in enrollment is highest during the desegregation implementation period, it does not necessarily follow that this is due to "white flight" from desegregation. It may be due to events occurring long before the desegregation plan.

AN ALTERNATIVE HYPOTHESIS

Having discovered that the most coercive types of desegregation plans are most successful at reducing segregation, the

Table 5.1 (continued)

Year	Montgomery County	Portland	Racine	St Paul	San Bernardino	San Diego	Springfield	Stockton	Tacoma	Tulsa
1964	--	--	--	--	--	--	--	--	--	--
1965	--	-0.6	--	--	--	--	--	--	--	--
1966	+0.2	-0.3	--	--	--	-0.9	+0.6	-0.5	--	--
1967	-0.3	-2.8	--	+0.4	--	-1.3	-0.6	+0.8	--	--
1968	-2.7	+0.1	-0.4	-0.1	--	0	-4.4	-2.4	-0.7	-4.9
1969	-0.9	+1.9	-0.7	-0.8	-0.7	-1.8	-1.9	-1.0	-0.7	-0.3
1970	-1.1	-3.4	-0.8	-0.7	-0.8	-0.3	-2.7	-0.7	-0.9	-0.4
1971	-0.7	-0.9	-0.1	-0.3	-1.3	-0.8	-2.4	-1.4	-0.9	-0.5
1972	-1.1	-1.1	-0.9	-0.5	-0.5	-1.5	-1.8	-0.8	-0.1	-1.9
1973	-0.3	-1.0	-0.3	-1.1	-1.0	-1.1	-2.7	-0.8	-0.8	-1.3
1974	-0.8	-0.6	-0.9	-0.9	-2.0	-0.9	-2.5	-2.7	-0.9	-2.0
1975	-1.3	-1.6	-0.5	-0.1	+0.6	-1.9	-2.3	-1.6	-1.7	-0.2
1976	-3.9	-1.2	-1.0	-2.0	+0.4	-1.8	-1.2	-2.8	-1.0	-0.7
1977	-0.7	-1.6	-1.3	-1.4	-2.2	-2.0	-2.4	-1.1	-0.3	-1.9
1978	-0.8	-1.5	-2.2	-2.2	-3.2	-2.3	-2.0	-3.0	-0.7	-1.6
1979	-1.6	-1.7	+0.3	-2.2	-2.7	-2.9	-1.2	-2.9	-2.0	-1.7
1980	-2.1	-0.8	-1.4	-3.6	-1.4	-3.5	-2.5	-1.8	-1.6	-1.1
1981	-2.1	-3.6	-1.1	-3.4	-1.7	-3.2	-1.1	-2.5	-1.4	-1.2
1982	-1.6	+0.4	-0.2	-2.3	-0.9	-1.8	-2.3	-2.1	-0.8	-0.6
1983	-1.6	+0.8	-0.9	-0.8	-1.5	-1.2	-1.7	-1.6	-0.8	-0.8
1984	-1.7	0	-1.2	-1.2	-0.9	-1.6	-0.4	-2.0	-0.2	-0.7
1985	-1.4	-0.1	-1.0	-1.4	-1.4	-1.2	-0.7	-1.4	-1.2	-0.7
1986	-1.4	-0.5	-1.3	-2.4	-1.0	-1.5	-0.3	-1.4	-0.8	-0.4
1987	-1.5	-0.1	-0.9	-1.1	-1.7	-1.8	-1.5	-0.9	0	-0.8
1988	-1.8	-0.4	-0.4	-1.8	-1.4	-1.6	-2.5	-1.1	-1.1	-0.1

controversial issue commonly called "white flight" needs to be addressed to determine whether or not the plans are undermined by whites fleeing desegregated schools. Simply examining the percentage losses in white enrollment may not be an adequate substitute for a more rigorous scrutiny (see Table 5.2).

One might expect a larger decrease in white enrollment in the High Level of Coercion category because it allows for the least amount of freedom for parents as to where their children attend school and may incite a greater amount of hostility as a result. Yet the data in Table 5.2 are not indicative of this. During the first year of implementation, the average decline in white enrollment is quite similar across intervention types, save for the High Level of Choice category, which may or may not be due to the small sample size.

Given these similarities, it seems plausible that there might be more to this issue than simply whites fleeing desegregation efforts. Perhaps the enrollment declines can be attributed to other factors. For example, it would follow that the number of white students in a school system would decrease if the available pool of white school-aged children decreased simultaneously. Thus, the key to understanding the level of white enrollment in school districts is to devise a method of estimating the number of white school-aged children in the city involved. A decline in the white birth rate would reduce the white enrollment in the schools. Other factors such as the migration of the middle and upper strata to suburbia would also impact enrollments in the central city schools.

ESTIMATING THE NUMBER OF WHITE SCHOOL-AGED CHILDREN

The U.S. census provides population figures by race and age every decade. During the time period used here, the 1960, 1970, and 1980 censuses act as a baseline by which the years in between each census can be estimated by adding the white births by residence, while factoring in infant mortality to arrive at a figure for white school-aged children (those between six and seventeen years old). These data are obtained from the *Vital Statistics of the United States.* The key is to arrive at an estimate of the white population between the ages of six and seventeen. By way of example, city A has 40,000 white children between these ages in 1970 and 20,000 in 1980. Arriving at estimates for 1971–79 is accomplished by using 1970 as the baseline. To be between six

Table 5.2
Means Analysis of Percentage Change in White Enrollment During the First Year of Implementation by Intervention Type

Category	Mean	Standard Deviation
High Level of Coercion (N=8)	-2.5	1.5
Moderate Level of Coercion with Low Level of Choice (N=6)	-2.1	1.4
Moderate Level of Choice with Low Level of Coercion (N=7)	-2.3	1.2
High Level of Choice (N=3)	-1.3	0.7

and seventeen years old in 1970, a student would have to be born between 1953 and 1964. Therefore, the following scenario exists:

Year	6–17 in Year X	U.S. Census Figure
1970	1953–1964	40,000
1971	1954–1965	40,000 plus:

1. add births in 1965,
2. subtract births in 1953, and
3. subtract infant mortality in 1965.

Upon doing this, say a figure of 37,000 is reached. In 1972, one would take this figure, add the births in 1966, subtract the births in 1954 as those in this group are no longer between six and seventeen (they are eighteen), and subtract infant mortality in 1966. A new figure is arrived at, and the process repeats itself until the following decade (1980). Upon reaching an estimate for school-aged children in 1980, this figure is compared to the census figure to determine the difference. This difference is attributed to either inward or outward migration, depending upon whether it is higher or lower than the census figure. Take the difference between the estimated figure and the census figure and divide by ten. This will provide an estimate of migration. Finally, the process is repeated, only this time the migration figure is calculated in as well.

A few assumptions are made by this formula—that the census figure is the most reliable estimate, and that during the years 1981–88, migratory practices will reflect those between

Table 5.3

Pearsonian Correlation Coefficients Between Estimated Number of Whites in the City Aged Six to Seventeen and White Enrollment in the Public Schools

Boston	.97	Montgomery	.95
Buffalo	.97	County	
Cincinnati	.96	Portland	.98
Dallas	.96	Racine	.98
Dayton	.93	St. Paul	.96
Des Moines	.98	San Bernardino	.99
Houston	.92	San Diego	.98
Jefferson	.97	Springfield	.99
County		*Stockton	-.39
Milwaukee	.99	Tacoma	.99
Montclair	.97	Tulsa	.98

*This is the only case where the correlation is < .92 and in an inverse direction. The estimated number of whites between 6–17 increased, while white enrollment in the public schools decreased. This may be due to a precipitous increase in the reported white birth rate in 1978–82, affecting the years 1984–88. When the years 1984–88 are omitted, the correlation becomes positive (.44), but is still significantly lower than the others.

1970–80. Since the complete 1990 census is not available yet, there is little choice but to utilize this estimate. Lastly, the formula assumes a constant rate of migration for each year during the decade. Some years may contain an economic boom or recession, which might impact the number of white families either moving in or out. Nevertheless, it is the best estimate available.

To determine the plausibility of these estimates, a correlation table is provided in Table 5.3. Correlations between the number of whites enrolled and the number of white people between six and seventeen should obviously be very high since one feeds on the other. The correlation coefficients seemingly lend some credence to the estimates, as in nineteen out of twenty cases, $r = .92$ or better.

White enrollment decreased because the available pool of school-aged children decreased, due to a declining birth rate among the white population as well as migratory practices over time. A few caveats should be mentioned. First, the estimates from 1980 forward appear to be too low. In many instances, trend lines are similar throughout until the 1980s. This leads one to believe that migration between 1970 and 1980 was proportionately greater than between 1980 and 1990. The 1990 census will either confirm or refute this conclusion.

Second, in basically two instances, white enrollment in the schools is higher than the number of available white school-aged children. This is counterintuitive, yet may have a viable explanation. First, this occurs in the mid- to late 1980s, frequently, and may be due to an overestimated migration figure as discussed above. This is especially noteworthy in Dayton, where the estimate approached zero by factoring in the migration behavior from 1970–80. The second instance relates mostly to the cities of Des Moines, Portland, Racine, San Bernardino, and Tacoma. Birth and mortality figures for several of the years had to be estimated by utilizing regression and trend analysis over time. It would seem that these techniques generated low figures. Regardless, the trend lines still reflect a similar pattern.

"WHITE FLIGHT" OR WHITE MIGRATION TO THE SUBURBS AND A LOWER BIRTH RATE?

If whites are fleeing desegregation plans, especially coercive ones, then the number of six to seventeen year olds during the implementation period should fall off sharply. Yet, irrespective of intervention type and implementation period, the decline in white school-aged children and enrollment has followed a steady, continual downward pattern. Stockton is the only deviation—the number of white school-aged children begins to increase in the mid-1980s as white enrollment decreases. As discussed earlier, this may be due in part to questionable birth data (see Table 5.3).

While the white population has vastly declined since 1960 in the majority of these cities, the nonwhite population has increased or remained fairly stable. The census figures in Table 5.4 illuminate this point. To argue that whites flee desegregation plans ignores a declining white birth rate over time as well as various socioeconomic factors that stimulate migration to the suburbs.

Table 5.4
U.S. Census Figures for Six to Seventeen Year Olds in Twenty Cities

City	Year	Total	White	(%Total)	Nonwhite	(%Total)
Boston	1960	122,490	107,789	88.0	14,701	12.0
	1970	121,485	90,240	74.3	31,245	25.7
	1980	85,999	45,176	52.5	40,823	47.5
Buffalo	1960	99,788	83,177	83.4	16,611	16.6
	1970	97,518	68,453	70.2	29,065	29.8
	1980	62,181	35,818	57.6	26,363	42.4
Cincinnati	1960	95,010	71,021	74.8	23,989	25.2
	1970	94,182	59,174	62.8	35,008	37.2
	1980	63,439	33,048	52.1	30,391	47.9
Dallas	1960	144,430	114,970	79.6	29,460	20.4
	1970	194,155	132,709	68.4	61,446	31.6
	1980	164,178	75,771	46.2	88,407	53.8
Dayton	1960	53,458	40,058	74.9	13,400	25.1
	1970	52,259	31,685	60.6	20,574	39.4
	1980	36,100	17,980	49.8	18,120	50.2
Des Moines	1960	42,380	39,831	94.0	2,549	6.0
	1970	43,757	40,261	92.0	3,496	8.0
	1980	32,960	28,230	85.6	4,730	14.4
Houston	1960	206,335	157,150	76.2	49,185	23.8
	1970	301,938	210,145	69.6	91,793	30.4
	1980	302,571	155,843	51.5	146,728	48.5
Jefferson	1960	135,768	118,130	87.0	17,638	13.0
County	1970	175,046	147,118	84.0	27,928	16.0
	1980	130,063	102,851	79.1	27,212	20.9
Milwaukee	1960	142,819	126,703	88.7	16,116	11.3
	1970	159,301	123,791	77.7	35,510	22.3
	1980	113,086	64,925	57.4	48,161	42.6
Montclair	1960	8,132	6,269	77.1	1,863	22.9
	1970	9,082	6,414	70.6	2,668	29.4
	1980	6,374	4,048	63.5	2,326	36.5
Montgomery	1960	86,644	83,305	96.1	3,339	3.9
County	1970	135,662	128,288	94.6	7,374	5.4
	1980	114,194	94,766	83.0	19,428	17.0
Portland	1960	72,613	67,684	93.2	4,929	6.8
	1970	74,176	66,300	89.4	7,876	10.6
	1980	51,883	40,510	78.1	11,373	21.9
Racine	1960	19,257	18,056	93.8	1,201	6.2
	1970	24,046	20,479	85.2	3,567	14.8
	1980	16,807	12,234	72.8	4,573	27.2
St. Paul	1960	63,395	61,162	96.5	2,233	3.5
	1970	66,676	62,734	94.1	3,942	5.9
	1980	43,217	36,011	83.3	7,206	16.7
San	1960	20,489	18,347	89.5	2,142	10.5
Bernardino	1970	24,438	18,929	77.5	5,509	22.5
	1980	21,562	12,208	56.6	9,354	43.4
San Diego	1960	112,674	102,936	91.4	9,738	8.6
	1970	146,823	125,891	85.7	20,932	14.3
	1980	144,675	96,385	66.2	48,290	33.8
Spring-	1960	34,785	31,646	91.0	3,139	9.0
field	1970	36,601	30,100	82.2	6,501	17.8
	1980	29,370	18,361	62.5	11,009	37.5
Stockton	1960	17,694	14,394	81.3	3,300	18.7
	1970	23,817	17,738	74.5	6,079	25.5
	1980	28,757	16,513	57.4	12,244	42.6
Tacoma	1960	32,188	30,295	94.1	1,893	5.9
	1970	35,377	30,825	87.1	4,552	12.9
	1980	28,198	21,837	77.4	6,361	22.6
Tulsa	1960	56,058	49,960	89.1	6,098	10.9
	1970	77,621	65,101	83.9	12,520	16.1
	1980	61,588	46,564	75.6	15,024	24.4

Large urban cities are often places where poverty and crime are usually quite apparent and thus not the ideal place of residence for many who can afford to live elsewhere. Since minorities are less affluent on average than whites, it should not be surprising that their migratory patterns differ. Whites have been leaving central cities for a number of years, and do not suddenly flee en masse when desegregation of the public schools becomes a reality. Maintaining otherwise ignores a great deal about a city's history before desegregation. In fact, given the reality of the overwhelmingly white suburbia, perhaps the current school desegregation debate needs to focus not only on techniques, but geography as well.

Chapter 6

Future Progress Toward Desegregation

SUMMARY OF FINDINGS

The analysis upholds the traditional New Deal liberal view that state intervention is justified when its purpose is to remedy conduct harmful in its consequences. In other words, if whites will not participate in desegregation voluntarily, then they must be coerced into doing so, because this behavior is harmful to the minority population. There is a constitutional issue involved (the Fourteenth Amendment Equal Protection Clause), as well as a plethora of sociological, political, and moral issues. The negative consequences of racism on minority groups are well documented. Segregation is also extremely harmful to whites because learned prejudicial behavior is difficult to overcome in environments dominated by the white majority population. Ignorance begets ignorance, and the vicious status quo is perpetuated.

The districts that employed the most coercive techniques of rezoning and pairing and/or clustering (along with magnet schools for reasons delineated in Chapter 3) fared better in terms of reducing segregation in their respective schools. These findings contradict some recent studies, most notably from Rossell (1990a, 1990b, 1988), and Rossell and Clarke (1987), which conclude that voluntary plans employing majority to minority transfers, magnet schools, and open enrollment achieve this goal best. Rossell's findings are based on her utilization of the Interracial Exposure Index as the ultimate dependent variable. The analysis presented here, however, relies upon the common measure of racial balance, the Index of Dissimilarity. *Smw* as a measure of segregation is deemed theoretically and statistically suspect, as it is used to measure two phenomena with a single indicator. First, it is used to measure the level of racial balance between differing racial groups. It does not do an adequate job at this because, while measures of dispersion quantify the deviation of a set of schools from a baseline of no segregation, measures of central tendency are not able to do this and simply reflect weighted averages such as the proportion of white students in the average minority child's school. Second, researchers utilizing measures of central tendency not only attempt to capture the racial mixing of students, but also attempt to reflect the mixing of students without losing them to assumed "white flight." The key word here is *assumed*. The analysis in Chapter 5 indicates that "white flight" is a faulty assumption in the first place. The reality is that whites have migrated to the more affluent suburbs for a number of years, irrespective of the type of desegregation intervention. The declining white birth rate is also well documented.

While noncoercive, voluntary desegregation efforts may be politically popular, they do not desegregate schools as well as mandated plans. The goal of desegregation is to reduce, and perhaps eliminate, racial imbalance. A full-fledged commitment to this goal would utilize the most successful intervention strategy—High Level of Coercion. Hochschild's (1984: 71) assertion is supported by rigorous data analysis with a sound measurement strategy. Since achieving racial balance is more effectively accomplished by utilizing a coercive intervention strategy, addressing the debate between the public choice model and the command and control model now becomes fruitful.

MODELS OF POLICY MAKING

The analysis of the four intervention types aids in understanding the debate between the public choice and command and control models (also called the conflict control model). The public choice model for school desegregation is based on the premise that most parents will make choices based on curricular incentives. Two assumptions are inherent in this model. First and primarily is that parents will rationally evaluate the educational program of the segregated neighborhood school and compare it to the desegregated magnet school. The secondary assumption is that a sufficient number of parents will opt for the magnet school because they perceive that their child will receive a "better" education there.

The command and control model assumes that coercion is necessary to induce white parents to take their children out of segregated schools. Although coercive techniques are utilized to do this, keep in mind that magnet schools are also established to reduce white hostility to the plan and to alleviate assumed "white flight." This is the case with all the districts in this study, for example.

The Public Choice Model

As Rossell (1990b: 20) reports, the idea of allowing elements of choice in school desegregation has its intellectual foundation in public choice theory. Inherent in this theory is the assumption that citizens will act in their own self-interest. The model assumes that state intervention is more effective when it restructures, rather than limits, the environment of choice. Utilizing this model, whites have the freedom to choose among a wide variety of alternatives, as they are the target population. They are in turn expected to act in a manner in their best interest. The state or governmental entity can encourage whites to desegregate through positive and negative incentives.

From her analysis, where desegregation is operationalized as interracial exposure, Rossell (1990b: 188) concludes that

the public choice model is now more effective than the command and control model. It is more efficient to try to change the behavior of citizens by restructuring the range of alternatives to choose from and encouraging socially desirable behavior through positive and negative incentives than it is to order the desegregation assignment of specific students to specific schools.

As a result, Rossell determines that magnet-only plans are more effective than plans with forced busing. Yet it is important to note that the term *busing* is appropriate for magnet-only plans and any other type of intervention as students are bused to school as a means of transportation, whether by choice or by imposition. Rossell delineates eight policy recommendations in favor of voluntary desegregation (1990b: 195–96):

1. Have racial controls on schools to promote the greatest desegregation via student transfers.

2. Locate magnet schools in predominantly minority neighborhoods so that whites will transfer to them.

3. Utilize majority to minority transfers with transportation costs covered by the school districts, with annual reenrollment guaranteed.

4. Provide for a wide variety of magnet programs available for the district's students.

5. Retain neighborhood schools and existing attendance zones.

6. Conduct a costly publicity campaign and student recruitment plan.

7. Implement districtwide desegregation goals.

8. Allow for ample time to achieve the goals of the desegregation plan.

The first two recommendations are fairly straightforward, given Rossell's findings. Transfers designed to provide for the most desegregation would have to be given top priority, considering the main goal. Secondly, magnets are usually most useful (for the purpose of desegregation) in minority neighborhoods. Given the findings in this research effort, however, several of her remaining recommendations would not be feasible for achieving optimum levels of desegregation.

In terms of techniques, it has been shown that the M to M transfer policy discussed in the third recommendation did not achieve as much desegregation as highly coercive techniques. Those districts in the High Level of Coercion category fared better than those in the High Level of Choice category in the criteria delineated in Chapter 4. The same assertion holds true for the fourth recommendation, since it is difficult to find a magnet school plan that does not have an M to M transfer program. The fifth point is also not supported by my data analysis. Rossell (1990b) calls for the retention of neighborhood schools and attendance zones. The results generated here lend credence to the opposite conclusion—that segregated neighborhood schools and their ensuing attendance areas need to be redrawn for the purpose of desegregating the schools.

Rossell's seventh recommendation is applicable to any type of intervention, whether it be a strategy providing for choice or coercion. If desegregation is the goal, then districts should opt for ambitious districtwide racial composition goals. Her other two points, however, are goals disputed by Hochschild (1984).

Hochschild objects to the expense of magnet school plans. As Rossell (1990b: 200) asserts, "voluntary plans that desegregate with magnet schools cost substantially more than mandatory plans with fewer magnet schools." The cost issue is not the focus of this work. However, since the analysis herein points to contrasting conclusions when compared to Rossell's recent works, it would appear that the added cost for magnet-dominated plans is not worth it, if the overriding purpose of the plan is to desegregate the district as much as possible. The eighth recommendation is also antithetical to the conclusions of many analysts. Rossell (1990b) supports an extended implementation period for voluntary efforts. This aspect of desegregation is not specifically addressed here, due to the concern of splitting each of the continuum categories further and thus possibly confronting the problem of less meaningful results as the number of cases would be decreased. By way of illustration, Hochschild (1984: 177) argues for "desegregation, full speed ahead," as the quicker the implementation period, the less harm for all parties involved.

The Command and Control Model

As Rossell (1990b) reports, the dominant model of policy making in the school desegregation literature and in the courts is the command and control model. Coercion is considered necessary in this model, because citizens are assumed to be refractory. In terms of specific interventions, desegregation plans are formulated with a limited range of choices. Specific students are assigned to specific schools for the purpose of desegregation. Unlike the public choice model, this model is based on the assumption that citizens are too consumed by racial prejudice to act in their own self-interest. A secondary assumption is that even if assumed "white flight" occurs, the net benefit to society is still greater than if the district relies upon voluntary transfers (Rossell, 1990b: 22).

Since the data analysis presented here substantiates the hypothesis that the most coercive plans are more effective than other intervention types, the command and control model is deemed more plausible than the public choice model. This implies that most citizens are motivated by attitudes formed during early socialization. Incentives in the form of magnet schools are not sufficient to lure them out of their segregated neighborhood schools. Simply put, they have to be coerced to do it.

Contemporary liberals take the position that state intervention is justified in order to alter behavior that is harmful to society. Certainly, discriminatory behavior is retrogressive to the minority population. On the basis of the data analysis, imposed change (i.e., those districts in the High Level of Coercion category) is more effective for the goal of desegregation. Side effects are not ignored in this study. Rossell's ultimate dependent variable assumes high levels of "white flight" from mandated desegregation. Yet the formula described in Chapter 5 contains useful information about the "white flight" hypothesis. A steady decline in the white population aged six to seventeen in central urban cities has been a trend for the past few decades, irrespective of desegregation intervention type.

While Hochschild (1984: 91) concludes that incremental policies in the form of voluntary transfers work poorly at desegregating schools, Rossell (1990b: 215) arrives at the opposite proposition: "More incremental policymaking works better than less incremental policymaking to desegregate schools because it causes less white flight and less citizen resentment." Two caveats should be mentioned here. First, white enrollment losses in the first year of implementation are strikingly similar irrespective of intervention type (see Chapter 5). Secondly, there may be other intervening factors during the implementation of any type of desegregation plan that may stimulate whites to leave the central cities. How much of the white enrollment losses during implementation is due to assumed "white flight"? That is a difficult question to address. The declining white birth rate is examined in Chapter 5, but surely other factors cause whites to migrate (namely, socioeconomic and class reasons). Since we know which types of interventions are more effective than others by utilizing a standard measure of segregation, the focus must now go beyond techniques to the issue of geographical settings.

A DIFFERENT FOCUS

Hochschild (1984: 190) argues that "wherever possible, desegregate a metropolitan region." Her point is noteworthy, as the decline in white enrollments in central cities, fueled by migration to the suburbs, has been continual for a number of years, to the point where the minority population in urban school districts is disproportionately higher than in the nation as a whole. She delineates the virtues of a metropolitan plan:

> It provides the flexibility needed for optimal ratios of race and class; it combines the resources and expectations of the suburbs

with the culture and excitement of the city; it minimizes white
flight and enhances stability and community support; it can
simplify busing logistics; it can foster and reward integrated
neighborhoods; it can break large districts into smaller, more
accessible units (1984: 190–91).

Obviously this remedy is not applicable to districts with a small
proportion of minorities and a large number of middle class
residents. Yet it would be practical in many settings. Consider the
success achieved by the merging of the Jefferson County public
schools and the Louisville Independent School District in Kentucky, for example.

Hochschild (1984: 191) explains the obstacles to metropolitan
desegregation. The first is fairly obvious. Such a policy would
face a strong public opposition from whites in the suburbs.
Elected public officials, as a result, would not likely support it
strongly, either. Since she argues that incremental policies designed to eliminate segregation are futile, following the popular
will will not adequately desegregate the public schools. Forcing
whites to desegregate is certainly not the ideal of liberalism, but
if real change is to be realized, coercive measures are both
necessary and justified.

The second obstacle would entail a virtual reversing of the
Milliken decision by the Supreme Court. As a result of this case,
suburbs can be ordered to participate in desegregation plans only
if they have practiced intentional segregation. As Hochschild
(1984) notes, these obstacles are not impossible to overcome.
Litigants involved in the judicial process could concentrate on
cities ripe for a metropolitan remedy; those outside the judicial
arena could work through state and local legislators or administrators. Whatever the scenario, albeit however difficult, there are
still concrete policy options to pursue to accomplish the goal at
hand.

The issue that remains is still Hochschild's (1984) "American
dilemma." Will effectual change be realized, benefiting many
while harming a few, or will the status quo be perpetuated, which

benefits a few at the expense of the many? Given the results of this study, the most feasible techniques are fairly straightforward; the willingness of administrators and political officials to apply them to a larger setting remains to be seen.

References

Albert, Geoffrey P.; White, H. Ron; and Geisel, Paul. 1981. "Dallas, Texas: The Intervention of Business Leaders." In Charles V. Willie and Susan L. Greenblatt (Eds.), *Community Politics and Educational Change: Ten School Systems Under Court Order*. New York: Longman, 155–73.

Armor, David J. 1980. "White Flight and the Future of School Desegregation." In Walter G. Stephan and Joe R. Feagin (Eds.), *School Desegregation: Past, Present, and Future*. New York: Plenum, 187–226.

Arrington, Karen McGill. 1981. *With All Deliberate Speed: 1954–19??* U.S. Commission on Civil Rights, Clearinghouse Publication 69. Washington, D.C.: U.S. Government Printing Office.

Barndt, Michael; Janka, Rick; and Rose, Harold. 1981. "Milwaukee, Wisconsin: Mobilization for School and Community Cooperation." In Charles V. Willie and Susan L. Greenblatt (Eds.), *Community Politics and Educational Change*, 237–59.

Bednarek, David I. 1977. "Milwaukee." *Integrated Education* 15, no.6, 36–37.

Bennett, David A. 1978. "Community Involvement in Desegregation: Milwaukee's Voluntary Plan." Paper presented at the 1978 annual meeting of the American Educational Research Association, March 27, 1978, Toronto, Ontario, Canada. ERIC Document ED 154 089.

———. 1984. "A Plan for Increasing Educational Opportunities and Improving Racial Balance in Milwaukee." In Charles V. Willie (Ed.), *School Desegregation Plans That Work.* Westport, Conn.: Greenwood Press, 81–118.

Bosco, James, and Robin, Stanley. 1974. "White Flight from Court-Ordered Busing?" *Urban Education* 9, no.1, 87–98.

———. 1976. "White Flight from Busing? A Second, Longer Look." *Urban Education* 11, no.3, 263–74.

Buell, Emmett, Jr., and Brisbin, Richard A., Jr. 1982. *School Desegregation and Defended Neighborhoods: The Boston Controversy.* Lexington: D.C. Heath.

Buffalo Evening News. April 30, 1976. Text of Judge Curtin's desegregation ruling, 11–14.

Buffalo Public Schools. N.d. *History of Desegregation in Buffalo.* Buffalo: Buffalo Public Schools.

———. May 18, 1976. *Buffalo Plan.* Buffalo: Buffalo Public Schools.

———. January 5, 1977. *Buffalo Plan: Phase II.* Buffalo: Buffalo Public Schools.

———. November 15, 1979. *Buffalo Public Schools: Desegregation Plan (Phase III).* Buffalo: Buffalo Public Schools.

———. January 27, 1981. *Buffalo Public Schools: Phase III (Revised).* Buffalo: Buffalo Public Schools.

Bullard, Pamela; Grant, Joyce; and Stoia, Judith. 1981. "Boston, Massachusetts: Ethnic Resistance to a Comprehensive Plan." In Charles V. Willie and Susan L. Greenblatt (Eds.), *Community Politics and Educational Change,* 31–63.

Bullard, Robert D. 1987. *Invisible Houston: The Black Experience in Boom and Bust.* College Station, Tex.: Texas A&M University Press.

Bullock, Charles, III. 1980. "The Office for Civil Rights and Implementation of Desegregation Programs in the Public Schools." *Policy Studies Journal* 8, no.4, 597–616.

Caldwell, Jean. May 21, 1975. "Springfield Hasn't Complied on Balance Plan, State Told." *The Boston Globe,* 20.

Campbell, Connie, and Brandsetter, John. 1977. "The Magnet School Plan in Houston." In Daniel U. Levine and Robert J. Havighurst (Eds.), *The Future of Big-City Schools: Desegre-*

gation Policies and Magnet Alternatives. Berkeley: McCutchan, 124–38.

Campbell, Donald T., and Stanley, Julian C. 1963. *Experimental and Quasi-Experimental Designs for Research.* Boston: Houghton Mifflin.

Case, Charles W. 1977. "History of the Desegregation Plan in Boston." In Daniel U. Levine and Robert J. Havighurst (Eds.), *The Future of Big-City Schools,* 153–76.

Cincinnati Public Schools, Department of Curriculum and Instruction. 1985. *Alternative Program and Open Enrollment Manual.* Bulletin No. 805. Cincinnati: Cincinnati Public Schools.

Clark, Karen. 1977. "Boston Desegregation: What Went Wrong?" *The Clearing House* 51, 157–59.

Clinchy, Evans. 1986. "Choice, Stability and Excellence: Parent and Professional Choice in Buffalo's Magnet Schools." *Equity and Choice* 2, no.3, 97–106.

Clotfelter, Charles T. 1978. "Alternative Measures of School Desegregation: A Methodological Note." *Land Economics* 54, no.3, 373–80.

Cohen, Muriel. 1977. Boston. *Integrated Education* 15, no.6, 9–10.

Coleman, James S. 1975. "Recent Trends in School Integration." *Educational Researcher* 4, 3–12.

Conference Before the United States Commission on Civil Rights. November 9, 1974. *Milliken v. Bradley: The Implications for Metropolitan Desegregation.* Washington, D.C.: U.S. Government Printing Office.

Conta, Dennis J. 1978. "Fiscal Incentives and Voluntary Integration: Wisconsin's Effort to Integrate Public Schools." *Journal of Education Finance* 3, 279–96.

Cook, Thomas D., and Campbell, Donald T. 1979. *Quasi-Experimentation: Design and Analysis Issues for Field Settings.* Boston: Houghton Mifflin.

Crain, Robert L., and Carsrud, Karen Banks. 1985. "The Role of the Social Sciences in School Desegregation Policy." In R. Lance Shotland and Melvin M. Mark (Eds.), *Social Science and Social Policy.* Beverly Hills: Sage, 219–36.

Cunningham, Claude H. 1978. "An Evaluation of Houston's Magnet School Program." Paper presented at the annual meeting of the American Educational Research Association, March 27–

31, 1978, Toronto, Ontario, Canada. ERIC Document ED 167 631.

———. 1980. "White Flight: A Closer Look at The Assumptions." *The Urban Review* 12, no.1, 23–30.

Dallas Independent School District. N.d.a. *Unitary Status: What Does It Mean and What Are Its Consequences.* Dallas: Dallas Independent School District.

———. N.d.b. *Desegregation Matrix, 1955 to 1976.* Dallas: Dallas Independent School District.

———. N.d.c. *Desegregation Matrix, 1976 and 1982 Orders.* Dallas: Dallas Independent School District.

Dayton Public Schools. January 6, 1989. Correspondence with Jill Moberley, ASPR Public Information Officer.

Dentler, Robert A. 1977. "Educational Implications of Desegregation in Boston." In Daniel U. Levine and Robert J. Havighurst (Eds.), *The Future of Big-City Schools*, 177–91.

———. 1978. "Desegregation Planning and Implementation in Boston." *Theory Into Practice* 17, no.1, 72–77.

———. 1984. "The Boston School Desegregation Plan." In Charles V. Willie (Ed.), *School Desegregation Plans That Work*, 59–80.

Dentler, Robert A., and Scott, Marvin B. 1981. *Schools On Trial: An Inside Account of the Boston Desegregation Case.* Cambridge: Abt Books.

Des Moines Public Schools. N.d. *Timeline of School Desegregation in the Des Moines Public Schools.* Des Moines: Des Moines Public Schools.

Edelman, Sandra. 1980. "Notes: The Segregative Impact of Changing Demographics Upon School Districts Subject to Court-Ordered Desegregation." *George Washington Law Review* 49, no.1, 100–122.

Farley, Reynolds. 1975. "Racial Integration in the Public Schools, 1967 to 1972." *Sociological Focus* 8, no.1, 3–26.

Farley, Reynolds; Richards, Toni; and Wurdock, Clarence. 1980. "School Desegregation and White Flight: An Investigation of Competing Models and Their Discrepant Findings." *Sociology of Education* 53, 123–39.

Fife, Brian L. Forthcoming. "In Defense of Mandated School Desegregation Plans: An Analysis of Kentucky's Jefferson County Experience." *Equity and Excellence.*

Foster, Gordon. 1973. "Desegregating Urban Schools: A Review of Techniques." *Harvard Educational Review* 43, no.1, 5–36.

Freedom House Institute on Schools and Education. February 22, 1975. *Boston Desegregation: The First Term, 1974–75 School Year.* Roxbury: Freedom House Institute on Schools and Education. ERIC Document ED 123 280.

Geddes, Elizabeth M. 1982. *Desegregation/Integration—Policies and Practices: Portland Public Schools, Portland, Oregon, 1970–1981.* Unpublished doctoral dissertation, Department of Educational Administration, Brigham Young University.

Giles, Michael W. 1974. "Measuring School Desegregation." *The Journal of Negro Education* 43, no.4, 517–23.

Giles, Michael W.; Gatlin, Douglas S.; and Cataldo, Everett F. 1974. "The Impact of Busing on White Flight." *Social Science Quarterly* 55, no.2, 493–501.

Giles, Michael W.; Cataldo, Everett F.; and Gatlin, Douglas S. 1975. "White Flight and Percent Black: The Tipping Point Reexamined." *Social Science Quarterly* 56 , no. 1, 85–92.

Glenn, Charles L., Jr. 1979. "State-Led Desegregation in Massachusetts." *Integrated Education* 17, 54–61.

Golightly, Cornelius L. 1963. "De Facto Segregation in Milwaukee Schools." *Integrated Education* 1, no.6, 27–31.

Goodwin, Procter, and Hoar. October 14, 1987. Memorandum to President and Members, Boston School Committee, and Superintendent of Schools, Laval S. Wilson.

Griffin, Virginia K. 1977. "Desegregation in Cincinnati: The Legal Background." In Daniel U. Levine and Robert J. Havighurst (Eds.), *The Future of Big-City Schools*, 87–94.

Gujarati, Damodar N. 1988. *Basic Econometrics.* New York: McGraw-Hill.

Harris, Ian M. 1983. "The Inequities Of Milwaukee's Plan." *Integrated Education* 21, nos.1–6, 173–177.

Hartzog, Ernest, and Thomas, Clint. 1979. *Board Resolution Responding to the Report of the Community Coalition for School Integration: A Progress Report.* Portland: Portland Public Schools, Community Relations and Staff Development Department.

Hawley, Willis D.; Rossell, Christine H.; and Crain, Robert L. 1983. "Directions for Future Research." In Christine H.

Rossell and Willis D. Hawley (Eds.), *The Consequences of School Desegregation*. Philadelphia: Temple University Press, 163–79.

Hawley, Willis D.; Crain, Robert L.; Rossell, Christine H.; Smylie, Mark A.; Fernandez, Ricardo R.; Schofield, Janet W.; Tompkins, Rachel; Trent, William T.; and Zlotnick, Marilyn S. 1983. *Strategies for Effective Desegregation: Lessons from Research.* Lexington: D.C. Heath.

Henderson, Ronald D.; von Euler, Mary; and Schneider, Jeffrey M. 1981. "Remedies for Segregation: Some Lessons from Research." *Educational Evaluation and Policy Analysis* 3, no.4, 67–76.

Henig, Jeffrey R. 1989. "Choice, Race, and Public Schools: The Adoption and Implementation of a Magnet Program." *Journal of Urban Affairs* 11, no.3, 243–59.

Hentschke, Guilbert C.; Lowe, William T.; and Royster, Eugene C. 1985. "School Desegregation Policy for the Next Thirty Years." *Urban Education* 20, no.2, 149–75.

Hillson, Jon. 1977. *The Battle of Boston*. New York: Pathfinder.

Hochschild, Jennifer L. 1984. *The New American Dilemma: Liberal Democracy and School Desegregation*. New Haven: Yale University Press.

Hula, Richard C. 1984. "Housing Market Effects of Public School Desegregation: The Case of Dallas, Texas." *Urban Affairs Quarterly* 19, no.3, 409–23.

James, David R., and Taeuber, Karl E. 1985. "Measures of Segregation." In Nancy Brandon Tuma (Ed.), *Sociological Methodology 1985*. San Francisco: Jossey-Bass, 1–32.

Jefferson County Public Schools. N.d. *History of Desegregation Plan Prior to April, 1984*. (Exhibit D). Louisville: Jefferson County Public Schools.

———. April 4, 1984. *Board of Education's Approved "Second Generation" Desegregation Plan*. (Exhibit E). Louisville: Jefferson County Public Schools.

———. September 29, 1989. Telephone Interview with Robert J. Rodosky, Director of Research.

Jones, Lanie. April 6, 1978. "San Diego Integration Ads Run Into Snags." *Los Angeles Times*, Part II, p. 1.

Josey, Leronia (Ed.). 1974. *Desegregation Resource Handbook*. Report to the Office of Education, Department of Health, Education, and Welfare (HEW). Philadelphia: Philadelphia School District, Office of Community Affairs. ERIC Document ED 103 500.

Jung, P. Michael. May 9, 1988. *A Brief History of the Dallas School Desegregation Cases*. Dallas: Dallas Independent School District.

Kelly, Patrick, and Miller, Will. 1989. "Assessing Desegregation Efforts: No 'Best Measure.' " *Public Administration Review* 49, no.5, 431-37.

Kentucky Commission on Human Rights. 1972. *Louisville School System Retreats to Segregation: A Report on Public Schools in Louisville, Kentucky, 1956-1971*. Louisville: Kentucky Commission on Human Rights.

Kritek, William J. 1977. "Voluntary Desegregation in Wisconsin." *Integrated Education* 16, 83-87.

Larson, John C. January 1980. *Takoma Park Magnet School Evaluation: 1977-1979 (Part I: A Desegregation Study)*. Rockville, Md. : Montgomery County Public Schools, Department of Educational Accountability.

Larson, John C., and Allen, Brenda A. January 1988. *A Microscope on Magnet Schools, 1983 to 1986: Pupil and Parent Outcomes (Vol. 2)*. Rockville, Md.: Montgomery County Public Schools, Department of Educational Accountability.

Larson, John C., and Kirshstein, Rita J. July 1986. *A Microscope on Magnet Schools, 1983 to 1985: Implementation and Racial Balance*. Rockville, Md.: Montgomery County Public Schools, Department of Educational Accountability.

Larson, John C.; Stallworth, William L.; and Tompkins, Leroy J. February 1981. *Takoma Park Magnet School Evaluation (Part II: Final Report)*. Rockville, Md.: Montgomery Public Schools, Department of Educational Accountability.

Levine, Daniel U., and Estes, Nolan. 1977. "Desegregation and Educational Reconstruction in the Dallas Public Schools." *Phi Delta Kappan* 59, no.3, 163-67, 221.

Levine, Daniel U., and Havighurst, Robert J. (Eds.). 1977. *The Future of Big-City Schools: Desegregation Policies and Magnet Alternatives*. Berkeley: McCutchan.

Lewis-Beck, Michael S., and Alford, John R. 1980. "Can Government Regulate Safety? The Coal Mine Example." *American Political Science Review* 74, 745–56.

Lord, J. Dennis. 1975. "School Busing and White Abandonment of Public Schools." *Southeastern Geographer* 15, no.2, 81–92.

Lord, J. Dennis, and Catau, John C. 1977. "School Desegregation Policy and Intra-School District Migration." *Social Science Quarterly* 57, no.4, 784–96.

Massachusetts Advisory Committee. January 1975. *Route 128: Boston's Road to Segregation.* Joint Report of the Massachusetts Advisory Committee to the U.S. Commission on Civil Rights and the Massachusetts Commission Against Discrimination.

Massachusetts Research Center. 1976. *Education and Enrollments: Boston During Phase II.* Boston: Massachusetts Research Center.

Milwaukee Public Schools. September 16, 1987. *Settlement Agreement Filed in the United States District Court, Eastern District of Wisconsin.* Milwaukee: Milwaukee Public Schools.

Minnesota Department of Education, Equal Educational Opportunities Section. N.d. *A Compilation of State and Federal Laws Prohibiting Discrimination.* St. Paul: Minnesota Department of Education, Equal Opportunities Section.

Montgomery County Public Schools. October 10, 1983. *A Policy Statement on Quality Integrated Education.* Rockville, Md.: Montgomery County Public Schools.

———. December 28, 1988. Correspondence with Dr. Sandra Robinson, Office of Magnet Programs.

Morgan, David R., and England, Robert E. 1982. "Large District School Desegregation: A Preliminary Assessment of Techniques." *Social Science Quarterly* 63, no. 4, 688–700.

Morgan, David R.; England, Robert E.; and Laverents, Dianna. 1982. *Desegregating Public Schools: A Handbook for Local Officials.* Bureau of Government Research, University of Oklahoma.

Muskal, Fred, and Treadwell, Donna. 1981. "Stockton, California: Education and Coalition Politics." In Charles V. Willie and Susan L. Greenblatt (Eds.), *Community Politics and Educational Change*, 298–315.

O'Grady, Michael J. 1986. *Desegregation and White Flight: A Quantitative Model Assessing the Relative Effectiveness of Desegregation Methods.* Unpublished doctoral dissertation, Department of Political Science, University of Rochester.

Ollie, Bert W., Jr. 1977. "Racine." *Integrated Education* 15, no.6, 24-27.

Orfield, Gary. 1977. "Policy Implications of Research on White Flight in Metropolitan Areas." In Daniel U. Levine and Robert J. Havighurst (Eds.), *The Future of Big-City Schools,* 70-84.

———. 1983. *Public School Desegregation in the United States, 1968-1980.* Washington, D.C.: Joint Center for Political Studies.

———. 1988. "School Desegregation in the 1980s." *Equity and Choice* 4, 25-28.

Parelius, Robert James. January 3, 1983. *Perspectives on Desegregation: A Report to the New Jersey Office of Equal Educational Opportunity.* Highland Park, N.J.: New Jersey Office of Equal Educational Opportunity.

Perley, Martin M. 1975. "The Louisville Story." *Integrated Education* 13, no.6, 11-14.

Pettigrew, Thomas F., and Green, Robert L. 1976. "School Desegregation in Large Cities: A Critique of the Coleman 'White Flight' Thesis." *Harvard Educational Review* 46, no.1, 1-53.

Portland Public Schools. N.d. *The Portland Magnet Project: Improving Racial Balance, Educational Quality, and Choice in the Portland Public Schools.* Portland: Portland Public Schools.

———. April 14, 1980. *Comprehensive Desegregation Plan.* Portland: Portland Public Schools.

———. October 26, 1981. *Desegregation Implementation Plan: Phase II.* Portland: Portland Public Schools.

Racine Unified School District. December 19, 1988. Correspondence with Jack V. Parker, Administrator for Planning, Information, and Research.

Ricewell and Patterson (Attorney's Office, Houston, Texas). January 19, 1989. Telephone Interview with Attorney Kelly Frels.

Riecken, Henry W., and Boruch, Robert F.(Eds.) 1974. *Social Experimentation: A Method for Planning and Evaluating Social Intervention.* New York: Academic.

Rist, Ray C. 1980. "On the Future of School Desegregation: A New American Dilemma?" In Walter G. Stephan and Joe R. Feagin (Eds.), *School Desegregation: Past, Present, and Future.* New York: Plenum, 117-31.

Roberts, Gary J., and George, Vivian G. May, 1986. "The Springfield Story: The History of Desegregation in Springfield Schools." Paper presented to the Diversity and Choice Conference, Worcester, Mass.

Roeser, Veronica A. 1968. "Notes: De Facto Segregation and the Law: Focus San Diego." *San Diego Law Review* 5, 57-82.

Rossell, Christine H. 1975a. "White Flight." *Integrated Education* 13, no.6, 3-10.

——. 1975b. "School Desegregation and White Flight." *Political Science Quarterly* 90, no.4, 675-95.

——. 1977a. "The Mayor's Role in School Desegregation Implementation." *Urban Education* 12, no.3, 247-70.

——. 1977b. "Boston's Desegregation and White Flight." *Integrated Education,* January/February, 36-39.

——. 1978. *Assessing the Unintended Impacts of Public Policy: School Desegregation and Resegregation.* ERIC Document ED 160 688.

——. 1979. "Magnet Schools as a Desegregation Tool: The Importance of Contextual Factors in Explaining Their Success." *Urban Education* 14, no.3, 303-320.

——. 1981. "Predicted and Actual Interracial Contact Pre and Post Desegregation in Boston, 1969-1980." Unpublished manuscript, Department of Political Science, Boston University.

——. 1983. "Applied Social Science Research: What Does It Say About the Effectiveness of School Desegregation Plans?" *Journal of Legal Studies* 12, 69-107.

——. 1985a. "Estimating the Net Benefit of School Desegregation Reassignments." *Educational Evaluation and Policy Analysis* 7, no.3, 217-27.

——. 1985b. "What Is Attractive About Magnet Schools?" *Urban Education* 20, no.1, 7-22.

——. 1988. "How Effective Are Voluntary Plans with Magnet Schools?" *Educational Evaluation and Policy Analysis* 10, no.4, 325-342.

————. 1990a. "The Carrot or the Stick for School Desegregation Policy?" *Urban Affairs Quarterly* 25, no.3, 474–99.

————. 1990b. *The Carrot or the Stick for School Desegregation Policy: Magnet Schools or Forced Busing?* Philadelphia: Temple University Press.

Rossell, Christine H., and Clarke, Ruth C. 1987. *The Carrot or the Stick in School Desegregation Policy?* Report to the National Institute of Education. ERIC Document ED 279 781.

Rossell, Christine H., and Hawley, Willis D. 1982. "Policy Alternatives for Minimizing White Flight." *Educational Evaluation and Policy Analysis* 4, no.2, 205–222.

————. (Eds.). 1983. *The Consequences of School Desegregation.* Philadelphia: Temple University Press.

Rossell, Christine H., and Ross, J. Michael. 1979. *The Long-Term Effect of Court-Ordered Desegregation on Student Enrollment in Central City Public School Systems: The Case of Boston, 1974–79.* Report prepared for the Boston School Department.

Rossell, Christine H.; Schofield, Janet W.; Crain, Robert L.; Mahard, Rita E.; Eyler, Janet; Cook, Valerie; Tompkins, Rachel; Trent, William T.; and Ward, Leslie. 1981. *A Review of the Empirical Research on Desegregation: Community Response, Race Relations, Academic Achievement and Resegregation.* Vol. V. Center for Education and Human Development Policy, Institute for Public Policy Studies, Vanderbilt University.

Royster, Eugene C.; Baltzell, D. Catherine; and Simmons, Fran Cheryll. 1979. *Study of the Emergency School Aid Act Magnet School Program.* Report prepared for the Office of Education, Department of Health, Education, and Welfare (HEW).

Saint Paul Public Schools. May 22, 1984. *Plans for Bringing Cited Schools into Compliance with State Board of Education Rules on Desegregation.* Saint Paul: Saint Paul Public Schools (Independent School District 625).

————. August 1984. *Desegregation/Integration Plan for the St. Paul Public Schools.* Saint Paul: Saint Paul Public Schools (Independent School District 625).

San Bernardino City Unified School District. October 26, 1972. *Desegregation and Integration Plan.* San Bernardino: San Bernardino City Unified School District.

―――. October 13, 1989. Telephone interview with Danny Ward, Director of Desegregation/Integration.

San Diego City Schools. October 13, 1989. Telephone interview with Sandra Robles, Administrative Assistant.

Sheehan, J. Brian. 1984. *The Boston School Integration Dispute: Social Change and Legal Maneuvers.* New York: Columbia University Press.

Smith, Ralph R. 1978. "Boston: Two Centuries and Twenty-Four Months: A Chronicle of the Struggle to Desegregate the Boston Public Schools." In Howard I. Kalodner and James J. Fishman (Eds.), *Limits of Justice: The Courts' Role in School Desegregation.* Cambridge, Mass.: Ballinger, 25-113.

Smylie, Mark A. 1983. "Reducing Racial Isolation in Large School Districts." *Urban Education* 17, no.4, 477-502.

Sorensen, Annemette; Taeuber, Karl E.; and Hollingsworth, Leslie J., Jr. 1975. "Indexes of Racial Residential Segregation for 109 Cities in the United States, 1940 to 1970." *Sociological Focus* 8, no.2, 125-42.

Springfield Public Schools. December 1, 1989. Telephone interview with Gary J. Roberts, Evaluator, Chapter 636 Programs.

Stephan, Walter G. 1980. "A Brief Historical Overview of School Desegregation." In Walter G. Stephan and Joe R. Feagin (Eds.), *School Desegregation* 3-23.

Stephan, Walter G., and Feagin, Joe R. (Eds.). 1980. *School Desegregation: Past, Present, and Future.* New York: Plenum.

Stockton Unified School District. April 6, 1976. *Return to Writ of Mandate: Desegregation Plan.* Stockton, Calif.: Stockton Unified School District.

―――. March 25, 1980. *Revised Desegregation Plan of the Stockton Unified School District.* Stockton, Calif.: Stockton Unified School District.

Tacoma Public Schools. January 23, 1989. Correspondence with James A. Laurent, Administrator for Research, Evaluation, and Instructional Support.

Taeuber, Karl E., and Taeuber, Alma F. 1965. *Negroes in Cities.* Chicago: Aldine.

Taylor, D. Garth. 1986. *Public Opinion and Collective Action: The Boston School Desegregation Conflict.* Chicago: University of Chicago Press.

Texas Education Agency. 1988. *Texas School Directory: 1988-89.*
Austin: Texas Education Agency.
Trombley, William. 1977a. "Houston." *Integrated Education* 15,
no.6, 92-94.
———. 1977b. "San Bernardino." *Integrated Education* 15, no.6,
103-04.
———. February 11, 1980. "Magnet Schools: Good Incentive to
Make Desegregation Work in San Bernardino." *Los Angeles
Times,* Part I, 8, 16-17.
Tufte, Edward R. 1974. *Data Analysis for Politics and Policy.* Engle-
wood Cliffs, N.J.: Prentice-Hall.
Tulsa Public Schools. October, 1986. *Neither Black Nor White: A
History of Integration in the Tulsa Public Schools, 1954-
1986.* Tulsa: Tulsa Public Schools.
United States Commission on Civil Rights. 1975. *Desegregating the
Boston Public Schools: A Crisis in Civic Responsibility.* Washington, D.C.: U.S. Government Printing Office.
———. 1976. *School Desegregation in Louisville and Jefferson
County, Kentucky.* Washington, D.C.: U.S. Government
Printing Office.
———. 1977a. *School Desegregation in Racine, Wisconsin.* Washington, D.C.: U.S. Government Printing Office.
———. 1977b. *School Desegregation in Portland, Oregon.* Washington, D.C.: U.S. Government Printing Office.
———. 1977c. *School Desegregation in Tulsa, Oklahoma.* Washington, D.C.: U.S. Government Printing Office.
———. 1977d. *Statement on Metropolitan School Desegregation.*
Washington, D.C.: U.S. Government Printing Office.
———. 1979a. *School Desegregation in Tacoma, Washington.* Washington, D.C.: U.S. Government Printing Office.
———. 1979b. *Desegregation of the Nation's Public Schools: A
Status Report.* Washington, D.C.: U.S. Government Printing
Office.
United States Department of Commerce, Bureau of the Census. 1961.
1960 Census of Population. Vol. 1pt. A. Washington, D.C.:
U.S. Government Printing Office.
———. 1973. *Characteristics of the Population.* Vol. 1, pts. 1 and
22. Washington, D.C.: U.S. Government Printing Office.

————. 1978. *County and City Data Book 1977*. Washington, D.C.: U.S. Government Printing Office.

————. 1983. *Characteristics of the Population*. Vol. 1. Washington, D.C.: U.S. Government Printing Office.

————. 1988. *County and City Data Book 1988*. Washington, D.C.: U.S. Government Printing Office.

————. Selected Years. *Current Population Reports*. Washington, D.C.: U.S. Government Printing Office.

United States Department of Education, Center for Education Statistics. Fall 1986. *Directory of Public Elementary and Secondary Education Statistics*. Washington, D.C.: U.S. Government Printing Office.

United States Department of Education, Office for Civil Rights. 1980. *Directory of Elementary and Secondary School Districts, and Schools in Selected School Districts: School Year 1978–1979*. Vols. I and II. Washington, D.C.: U.S. Government Printing Office.

United States Department of Health and Human Services, Office of Health, Research, Statistics, and Technology (National Center for Health Statistics). 1976–1985. *Vital Statistics of the United States*. Vol. I: Natality. Washington, D.C.: U.S. Government Printing Office.

United States Department of Health, Education, and Welfare, National Center for Health Statistics/Public Health Service. 1940–1975. *Vital Statistics of the United States*. Vol. I: Natality. Washington, D.C.: U.S. Government Printing Office.

United States Department of Health, Education, and Welfare, Office for Civil Rights. 1971, 1972, and 1973. *Directory of Public Elementary and Secondary Schools in Selected Districts: Enrollment and Staff by Racial/Ethnic Group: Fall 1968, 1970, and 1972*, respectively. Washington, D.C.: U.S. Government Printing Office.

————. 1979. *Directory of Elementary and Secondary School Districts, and Schools in Selected School Districts: School Year 1976–1977*. Vols. I and II. Washington, D.C.: U.S. Government Printing Office.

United States Department of Health, Education, and Welfare, Office of Education. 1969. *Directory: Public Elementary and Secondary Schools in Large School Districts: With Enrollment and Instructional Staff, by Race: Fall 1967*. Washington, D.C.: U.S. Government Printing Office.

von Euler, Mary, and Parham, David L. 1978. *A Citizen's Guide to School Desegregation Law*. ERIC Document ED 160 689.

Wegmann, Robert G. 1977. "Desegregation and Resegregation: A Review of the Research on White Flight from Urban Areas." In Daniel U. Levine and Robert J. Havighurst (Eds.), *The Future of Big-City Schools*, 11–54.

Weinberg, Meyer. 1975. "A Critique of Coleman." *Integrated Education* 13, no.4, 3–7.

———. 1977. "Desegregation and the Movement of People." *Research Review of Equal Education* 1, 18–33.

Welch, Finis, and Light, Audrey. 1987. *New Evidence on School Desegregation*. Prepared for the United States Commission on Civil Rights by the Unicon Research Corporation of Los Angeles. Clearinghouse Publication 92. Washington, D.C.: U.S. Government Printing Office.

Weldin, Charles E. 1977. *A Historical Study of the Development of Desegregation and Concomitant Curriculum/Organizational Changes in the Elementary Schools of St. Paul, Minnesota: 1964–1976*. Unpublished doctoral dissertation, Department of Education, University of Kansas.

Wen, Patricia. February 28, 1989. "Student Plan OK'd; Legal Fight Vowed." *The Boston Globe*, 1, 12.

Willie, Charles V. 1982. "Desegregation in Big-City School Systems." *The Educational Forum* 47, no.1, 83–96.

———. (Ed.) 1984. *School Desegregation Plans That Work*. Westport, Conn.: Greenwood Press.

Willie, Charles V., and Fultz, Michael. 1984. "Do Mandatory School Desegregation Plans Foster White Flight?" In Charles V. Willie (Ed.), *School Desegregation Plans That Work*, 163–71.

Willie, Charles V., and Greenblatt, Susan L. (Eds.). 1981. *Community Politics and Educational Change: Ten School Systems Under Court Order*. New York: Longman.

Wisconsin Department of Public Instruction. July 1988. *A Background Paper on the Milwaukee Settlement*. Madison: Wisconsin Department of Public Instruction.

Wurdock, Clarence. 1979. "Public School Resegregation After Desegregation: Some Preliminary Findings." *Sociological Focus* 12, no.4, 263–74.

Zlotnick, Marilyn S. 1981. *Assessment of Current Knowledge About the Effectiveness of School Desegregation Strategies.* Vol. 9. Nashville: Vanderbilt University, Center for Education and Human Development Policy. ERIC Document ED 212 727.

Zoloth, Barbara S. 1976. "Alternative Measures of School Segregation." *Land Economics* 52, no.3, 278–98.

COURT CASES

Landmark Supreme Court Cases

Plessy v. Ferguson, 163 U.S. 537, 41 L.Ed. 256, 16 S. Ct. 1138 (1896).

Brown v. Board of Education of Topeka, Kansas (Brown I), 347 U.S. 483, 98 L.Ed. 873, 74 S. Ct. 686 (1954).

Brown v. Board of Education of Topeka, Kansas (Brown II), 349 U.S. 294, 99 L.Ed. 1083, 75 S. Ct. 753 (1955).

Green v. County School Board of New Kent County, Virginia, 391 U.S. 430, 20 L.Ed. 2d 716, 88 S. Ct. 1689 (1968).

Swann v. Charlotte-Mecklenberg Board of Education, 402 U.S. 1, 28 L.Ed. 2d 554, 91 S. Ct. 1267 (1971).

Keyes v. School District No.1, Denver, Colorado, 413 U.S. 189, 37 L.Ed. 2d 548, 93 S. Ct. 2686 (1973).

Milliken v. Bradley, 418 U.S. 717, 41 L.Ed. 2d 1069, 94 S. Ct. 3112 (1974).

Boston, Massachusetts (Boston Public Schools)

Reported Opinions

School Committee of Boston v. Board of Education, 363 Mass. 20 (1973).

School Committee of Boston v. Board of Education, 363 Mass. 125 (1973).

School Committee of Boston v. Board of Education, 364 Mass. 199 (1973).

Morgan v. Hennigan, 379 F. Supp. 410 (D. Mass. 1974).

Morgan v. Kerrigan, 509 F.2d 580 (1st Cir. 1974).

Morgan v. Kerrigan, 401 F. Supp. 216 (D. Mass. 1975).

Morgan v. Kerrigan, 530 F.2d 401 (1st Cir. 1976).

Morgan v. McDonough, 689 F.2d 265 (1st Cir. 1982).

Unreported Opinions

Morgan v. Kerrigan, U.S. District Court, D. Mass., May 10, 1975. (Student Desegregation Plan) No. 72-911-G.

Morgan v. Nucci, U.S. District Court, D. Mass., September 3, 1985. (UFP Orders) No. 72-911-G.

Morgan v. Nucci, U.S. District Court, D. Mass., September 3, 1985. (Final Orders) No. 72-911-G.

Buffalo, New York (Buffalo Public Schools)

Reported Opinions

Arthur v. Nyquist, 415 F. Supp. 904 (W.D.N.Y. 1976).

Arthur v. Nyquist, 547 F.2d 7 (2d Cir. 1976).

Arthur v. Nyquist, 429 F. Supp. 206 (W.D.N.Y. 1977).

Arthur v. Nyquist, 573 F.2d 134 (2d Cir. 1978).

Cincinnati, Ohio (Cincinnati Public Schools)

Reported Opinions

Board of Education of the City School District of the City of Cincinnati v. Department of Health, Education, and Welfare, Region 5, 396 F. Supp. 203 (S.D. Oh. 1975).

Bronson v. Board of Education of the City School District of Cincinnati, 525 F.2d 344 (6th Cir. 1975).

*Board of Education of the City School District of the City of Cincinnati
v. Department of Health, Education, and Welfare, Region 5,* 532
F.2d 1070 (6th Cir. 1976).

*Bronson v. Board of Education of the City School District of the City
of Cincinnati,* 604 F. Supp. 68 (S.D. Oh. 1984).

Dallas, Texas (Dallas Independent School District)

Reported Opinions

Tasby v. Estes, 342 F. Supp. 945 (N.D. Tex. 1971).

Tasby v. Estes, 412 F. Supp. 1185 (N.D. Tex. 1975).

Tasby v. Estes, 517 F.2d 92 (5th Cir. 1975).

Tasby v. Estes, 412 F. Supp. 1192 (N.D. Tex. 1976).

Tasby v. Estes, 572 F.2d 1010 (5th Cir. 1978).

Tasby v. Wright, 542 F. Supp. 134 (N.D. Tex. 1981).

Tasby v. Wright, 585 F. Supp. 453 (N.D. Tex. 1984).

Tasby v. Black Coalition to Maximize Education, 771 F.2d 849 (5th Cir.
1985).

Tasby v. Wright, 630 F. Supp. 597 (N.D. Tex. 1986).

Dayton, Ohio (Dayton Public Schools)

Reported Opinions

Board of Education of School District of Dayton v. State ex rel. Reese,
114 Ohio St. 188, 189, 151 N.E. 39 (1926).

Brinkman v. Gilligan, 503 F.2d 684 (6th Cir. 1974).

Brinkman v. Gilligan, 518 F.2d 853 (6th Cir. 1975).

Brinkman v. Gilligan, 539 F.2d 1084 (6th Cir. 1976).

Dayton Board of Education v. Brinkman (Dayton I), 433 U.S. 406, 53
L.Ed. 2d 851, 97 S. Ct. 2766 (1977).

Brinkman v. Gilligan, 446 F. Supp. 1232 (S.D. Oh. 1977).

Brinkman v. Gilligan, 583 F.2d 243 (6th Cir. 1978).

Dayton Board of Education v. Brinkman (Dayton II), 443 U.S. 526, 61
L.Ed. 2d 720, 99 S. Ct. 2971 (1979).

Houston, Texas (Houston Independent School District)

Reported Opinions

Ross v. Eckels, 317 F. Supp. 512 (S.D. Tex. 1970).

Ross v. Eckels, 434 F.2d 1140 (5th Cir. 1970).

Ross v. Houston Independent School District, 457 F. Supp. 18 (S.D. Tex. 1977).

Ross v. Houston Independent School District, 559 F.2d 937 (5th Cir. 1977).

Ross v. Houston Independent School District, 583 F.2d 712 (5th Cir. 1978).

Ross v. Houston Independent School District, 699 F.2d 218 (5th Cir. 1983).

Unreported Opinions

Ross v. Eckels, U.S. District Court, S.D. Tex., Houston Div., September 18, 1970. (Amended Decree) No. 10444.

Ross v. Eckels, U.S. District Court, S.D. Tex., Houston Div., August 6, 1971. (Memorandum) No. 10444.

Ross v. Houston Independent School District, U.S. District Court, S.D. Tex., Houston Div., April 4, 1973. (Memorandum And Order) No. 10444.

Ross v. Houston Independent School District, U.S. District Court, S.D. Tex., Houston Div., April 27, 1973. (Injunction Decree) No. 10444.

Ross v. Houston Independent School District, U.S. District Court, S.D. Tex., Houston Div., July 11, 1975. (Order Amending Decree) No. 10444.

Ross v. Houston Independent School District, U.S. District Court, S.D. Tex., Houston Div., December 8, 1977. (Injunction Decree) No. 10444.

Ross v. Houston Independent School District, U.S. District Court, S.D. Tex., Houston Div., June 10, 1980. (Memorandum And Order) No. 10444.

Ross v. Houston Independent School District, U.S. District Court, S.D. Tex., Houston Div., June 17, 1981. (Memorandum And Order) No. 10444.

Ross v. Houston Independent School District, U.S. District Court, S.D. Tex., Houston Div., September 10, 1984. (Settlement Agreement) No. 10444.

Ross v. Houston Independent School District, U.S. District Court, S.D. Tex., Houston Div., November 27, 1984. (Order Approving Settlement Agreement) No. 10444.

Jefferson County/Louisville, Kentucky (Jefferson County Public Schools)

Reported Opinions

Newburg Area Council, Inc. v. Board of Education of Jefferson County, Kentucky, 489 F.2d 925 (6th Cir. 1973).

Newburg Area Council, Inc. v. Board of Education of Jefferson County, Kentucky, 510 F.2d 1358 (6th Cir. 1974).

Newburg Area Council, Inc. v. Board of Education of Jefferson County, Kentucky, 521 F.2d 578 (6th Cir. 1975).

Cunningham v. Grayson, 541 F.2d 538 (6th Cir. 1976).

Haycraft v. Board of Education of Jefferson County, Kentucky, 585 F.2d 803 (6th Cir. 1978).

Unreported Opinion

Newburg Area Council, Inc. v. Board of Education of Jefferson County, U.S. District Court, W.D. Ky., Louisville, July 3, 1975. Nos. 7045 and 7291 (Exhibit A).

Milwaukee, Wisconsin (Milwaukee Public Schools)

Reported Opinions

Amos v. Board of School Directors of the City of Milwaukee, 408 F. Supp. 765 (E.D. Wi. 1976).

Armstrong v. O'Connell, 416 F. Supp. 1344 (E.D. Wi. 1976).

Armstrong v. Brennan, 539 F.2d 625 (7th Cir. 1976).

Armstrong v. O'Connell, 451 F. Supp. 817 (E.D. Wi. 1978).

Armstrong v. Board of School Directors of the City of Milwaukee, 471 F. Supp. 800 (E.D. Wi. 1979).

Board of School Directors of the City of Milwaukee v. State of Wisconsin, 102 F.R.D. 596 (E.D. Wi. 1984).

San Bernardino, California (San Bernardino Unified School District)

Reported Opinions

Crawford v. Board of Education of the City of Los Angeles, 17 C.3d 280, 130 Cal. Rptr. 724, 551 P.2d 28 (1976).

NAACP v. San Bernardino City Unified School District, 46 Cal. App. 3d 49, 119 Cal. Rptr. 784, 551 P.2d 48 (1975).

NAACP San Bernardino City Unified School District, 17 C.3d 311, 130 Cal. Rptr. 744, 551 P.2d 48 (1976).

Unreported Opinion

NAACP v. San Bernardino City Unified School District, Superior Court of California, County of San Bernardino, September 13, 1973. (Judgment For Petitioners) No. 155286.

San Diego, California (San Diego Unified School District)

Reported Opinions

Crawford v. Board of Education of the City of Los Angeles, 17 C.3d 280, 130 Cal. Rptr. 724, 551 P.2d 28 (1976).

Unreported Opinions

Carlin v. Board of Education, Superior Court of California, County of San Diego, March 9, 1977. (Memorandum Decision And Order) No. 303800.

Carlin v. Board of Education, San Diego Unified School District, Superior Court of California, County of San Diego, November 4, 1983. (Order Re Integration Plan: 1983–84) No. 303800.

Springfield, Massachusetts (Springfield Public Schools)

Reported Opinions

Barksdale v. Springfield School Committee, 237 F. Supp. 543 (D. Mass. 1965).

Springfield School Committee v. Barksdale, 348 F.2d 261 (1st Cir. 1965).

School Committee of Springfield v. Board of Education, 362 Mass. 417 (1972).

School Committee of Springfield v. Board of Education, 365 Ma. 215 (1974).

Stockton, California (Stockton Unified School District)

Unreported Opinions

Hernandez v. Board of Education of the Stockton Unified School District, Superior Court of California, County of San Joaquin, October 4, 1976. (Order Denying Motions) No. 101016.

Hernandez v. Board of Education, Superior Court of California, County of San Joaquin, March 4, 1977. (Memorandum Of Decision) No. 101016.

Hernandez v. Board of Education of Stockton Unified School District, Superior Court of California, County of San Joaquin, April 27, 1978. (Judgment) No. 101016.

Tulsa, Oklahoma (Tulsa Public Schools)

Reported Opinions

U.S. v. Board of Education, Independent School District No.1, Tulsa County, Oklahoma, 429 F.2d 1253 (10th Cir. 1970).

U.S. v. Board of Education, Independent School District No.1, Tulsa County, Oklahoma, 459 F.2d 720 (10th Cir. 1972).

U.S. v. Board of Education, Independent School District No.1, Tulsa County, Oklahoma, 476 F.2d 621 (10th Cir. 1973).

Unreported Opinion

U.S. v. Board of Education, Independent School District No. 1 of Tulsa County, Oklahoma, U.S. District Court, N.D. Okla., November 9, 1983. (Order Closing Case) No. 68–C-185–D.

Index

About the Author

BRIAN L. FIFE is Assistant Professor of Political Science at Ball State University in Indiana. His current research focus is on urban public school desegregation. He has published in *Equity and Excellence* and *Knowledge: Creation, Diffusion, Utilization.*